MW00809683

A. Núñez

JOSE POLICARPO RODRIGUEZ.

JOSE POLICARPO RODRIGUEZ

"THE OLD GUIDE"

SURVEYOR, SCOUT, HUNTER, INDIAN FICHTER, RANCHMAN, PREACHER

HIS LIFE IN HIS OWN WORDS

Nashville, Tenn.; Dallas, Tex.
Publishing House of the Methodist Episcopal Church, South
Smith & Lamar, Agents

CONTENTS.

CHAPTER I.

(3)

187135 .

CHAPTER XI.

CHAPTER XII.

CHAPTER XIII.

CHAPTER XIV.

CHAPTER XV.

CHAPTER XVI.

CHAPTER XVII.

CHAPTER XVIII.

CHAPTER XIX.

CHAPTER XX.

CHAPTER XXI.

CHAPTER XXII.

INTRODUCTORY NOTE.

THIS story as follows was dictated to the Rev. D. W. Carter, D.D., at odd times during the years from 1892 to 1897. The unrevised manuscript was by him intrusted to me to be published; a work he could not attend to personally, owing to his arduous duties as a foreign missionary and consequent absence from the United States. I have thought it best to leave my friend's work exactly as first written down, correcting only a few obvious slips and eliminating repetitions. The colloquialisms will not offend most readers. Many slight turns of expression are due to the fact that Spanish, not English, is the narrator's native tongue.   G. B. WINTON.

JOSE POLICARPO RODRIGUEZ.

CHAPTER I.

BOYHOOD DAYS.

MANY of my friends have asked me to tell the story of my life, and I have consented to do so in the hope that it may prove interesting to them and not entirely valueless for other reasons.

It deals with conditions that have passed away, but which were thrilling and important in the early history of Texas. I have lived in Texas when it was a part of Mexico, when it was an independent republic, while it was one of the Confederate States, and hope to lay my body to rest in its soil in sight of Polly's Peak when my journey is ended.

I was born at Zaragoza, Mexico, thirty-five miles west of Eagle Pass, Tex., January 26, 1829. My father was José Antonio Rodriguez; my mother, Encarnacion Sanchez. My father was a man of means and well educated for his day; he lost much property by the depredations of wild Indians that then infested the country. He was desirous of educating me for the priesthood of the Romish Church; he made three separate attempts to put me in a seminary to educate me for that purpose, but failed, as at each time his plans were broken up by the revolutions which were

(7)

then so frequent. At the age of six he put me in a school at Nadadores, Coahuila, where I remained about eight months; thence I was taken to Cuatro Ciénegas, where I remained some six months. This was all the schooling I ever received, but my father taught me at home as occasion permitted.

In my twelfth year my father brought me to San Antonio, Tex., and apprenticed me to Jim Goodman to learn the trade of gunsmith. There I remained three years. Goodman killed a man, and was imprisoned; this ended my apprenticeship.

In the meantime my father had moved to Texas, near San Antonio, having bought a place on the Medina River, fifteen miles below town. San Antonio was then a very small place, consisting chiefly of straw-thatched *jacales*. I have played in the high weeds on the river where Commerce Street bridge now crosses. The Indians at that time often came into the town and stole horses, and had been known to kill people in the streets and carry off small boys. I hunted rabbits in the bend of the river between Houston and Commerce Streets. It was difficult at times to bury the dead in the cemetery where Milam Park now is, for fear of the prowling Indians.

At the end of my apprenticeship, I joined a party of surveyors, a Mr. Tivy, a gunsmith, in charge. A man named Goodman accompanied this party, which operated around where Boerne now stands. The country was then full of game animals and wild cattle; bear, deer, and turkeys especially abounded; the party lived on wild meat. Bee trees were common, and the surveyors had plenty of honey.

On one occasion when out on this survey we were surprised to see a party of Indians coming directly toward us. The only weapon we had with us was one old five-shooter pistol, we having left all our guns in camp. We squatted on the ground and crawled to a neighboring thicket through the tall grass. When the Indians came within half a mile of us they turned to the left and the party divided, some going by the mountain side and others continuing in the direction of San Antonio. Had they found our marks, they would have hunted for us, and we should have perished there. After this we did not go out without horses and arms.

CHAPTER II.

SURVEYING.

On this trip, at a big cave spring on the Guadalupe below Boerne, we were one day resting, when one of the party, looking into the cave, said, "I believe the devil is here," and gave a yell. Out rushed a big, fat black bear, splashing the water and scattering us from side to side; so scared were we that we forgot our guns and let him get away. We afterwards saw a bear passing with three young cubs, and went out and killed two of the cubs. I never tasted finer meat than young bear. After the survey was finished, we returned to San Antonio. I received the wages of a man—one dollar a day—though but fifteen years old. I could shoot and hunt and work on the survey as

well as a man. When we were beginning to carry
the chain, one of the men asked Mr. Tivy who was
going to carry the chain with him, and he said, "That
boy there," meaning me.

The man said: "I won't carry a chain with a boy."

"You won't?"

"No."

"Why?"

"Because he is nothing but a boy, and I won't work
with him."

"Then you can go. I'm responsible here, and that
boy can carry a chain as well as you can, and can
do things that you can't."

So he consented, and was one of my best friends
afterwards. From this time I went often with surveyors, as they seemed to pick me for such work. I
went with Mr. Zepher and with Mr. Bingham and
others.

In San Antonio in 1846 I bought my first horse, and
one night with a young fellow who had found a mule
lost by the Indians and another boy went hunting turkeys at the head of the San Antonio River. It was
drizzling rain, and we built a fire and passed the night
mainly in talk. Our horses were tied in the brush
near by, and the Indians came and stole them. We
went to General Harney and asked him for soldiers
to go with us to get our horses, but he refused.
Another boy and I went and followed them, but did
not find them. As we were but two, we thought it
dangerous to follow too far, and returned home.
So I lost my first horse, to which I was much attached. The boy who went with me after the horse

was Jacob Lynn, a German boy raised by a Mexican woman of San Antonio. He was the best shot I ever saw without exception. He could shoot a flying duck with a rifle. And I never saw a braver man than he became.

We went hunting once from San Antonio to Bandera County. We had four horses and six dogs. We killed several deer, a number of turkeys, one bear, and cut several bee trees. We found a bunch of wild cattle, most of them black or brown. We got after one and killed her. We emptied our guns into that cow before we killed her. Lynn had an eight-shooting pistol he had made himself, a rifle, and a pair of holsters; I had a rifle, a six-shooter, and a pair of holsters. Twenty shots went into the body of that black cow before we killed her. Then we camped. The Indians heard our shooting and came toward our camp, which was in a clump of small trees. We had had supper, fed our dogs plenty of beef, and had lain down to rest. Suddenly the dogs jumped up and ran out as if some one were coming, and we heard somebody talking low. We thought sure it was Indians, and we hissed on the dogs in English. The dogs ran out farther and barked as if they had something at bay. We hallooed loud and hissed the dogs. The Indians could not see how many there were of us, and feared to come on us. They thought there was a crowd of us, as we had fired very rapidly at the cow. The Indians stayed around us all night, but feared to charge us. They marched around and around us. They made all kinds of animal calls and cries. They were at one time barking like wolves, then hooting like owls, then fighting like wild cats or quacking like ducks. They thus tried to decoy us out or get us to expose ourselves, but we lay low. The Indians were all afoot, as we found out next morning. There were twenty or thirty of them, as the trail would indicate. Just before daylight we heard them leave. After we found that they were afoot, we decided to follow them, and found where they had killed a deer. They carried away every particle of the deer except the heart. We followed this trail until we saw the smoke rising from the bushes on a little hill, and decided that there were too many of them for us to attack, although we were well mounted and armed. They went on, and we thought it best to go home. We learned later that that party of Indians had killed four men—Germans—on the Medina, who were camped making shingles. They cut open their breasts and took out their hearts. They seemed to have some superstition about the heart. They left the deer's heart, but cut out and carried away the hearts of the men.

CHAPTER III.

Hunting Adventures.

Jacob Lynn and I, with a number of others, went hunting on the Medina Christmas, 1847. I took an ox cart to haul our game. Game was very plentiful, and we had wonderful success.

While my father lived on the Medina I was once coming to town (San Antonio) with a load of wood.

My aunt accompanied me. My dog scented the trail
of some animal and, following it, began to bark. I
took my gun and, following, found that he had treed
a panther. It was on a willow tree which overhung
the Leon Creek. I took aim at his head and fired.
It was not a dead shot, but the animal dropped into
the water, which was deep at that place, and began
to swim around. My dog jumped in after it, and
they clinched and both sank. To save my dog I took
off my clothes as quickly as possible and jumped into
the water. They came up both nearly drowned. The
dog swam one way and the panther the other. I
caught the panther by the tail and lifted it up so as to
sink his head in the water, and we swam around and
around, he trying to get at me and I keeping out of
his way. I got to where I could stand on the bottom,
and, holding up his tail, soon drowned him and took
his hide.

One Sunday a party of us (Lynn, Goodman, Matias,
Carrillo, and I) went deer-hunting near where West
End (San Antonio) now is, to the left of General
Russ's ranch. We saw some deer grazing ahead of
us, and I begged them to let me slip up and get a
shot. I crawled through the grass, and when not far
from a deer I saw all at once that it jumped, though
it had not seen me. It ran, and with several others
came toward me. I looked beyond, and saw a horse
and a man looking over the saddle. I thought he
was an Indian, and knew that if I emptied my gun
he would probably rush upon me and kill me. So I did
not shoot, though the deer were within a few feet of
me. I went back to the party, and I must have looked

scared, for they said: "What's the matter? Why didn't you kill the deer? You were close to it."

I said: "There is somebody there, and I think it is an Indian."

"You are a coward," said Matias; "it's nothing but a cow; I saw it go into the brush."

"Well, come with me, and we'll get the cow."

We all charged the thicket, and three mounted Indians ran out. We followed them, and I said to Matias: "Come on, and help get that cow!" But he hung back; he was the coward. Lynn and I chased those Indians three miles, but Matias stayed far behind. Lynn afterwards said to him: "You coward, we'll never come out with you again. I won't hunt with any man who's a coward." (Lynn was much younger than he.)

Some time after this Lynn and I again went hunting. We started out Saturday night, intending to return next day. When about two miles beyond San Pedro Springs, riding along in the bright moonlight, all at once our horses showed great signs of fear, and began shying and jumping. Lynn said: "Something is wrong."

I looked around, and saw off to our left a man come to the top of a hill. Then another and another, until seven were in sight, all Indians. "Let's run," said Lynn.

"No," said I; "if we do, they will shoot at us. Let us turn to the right, and go diagonally by them."

We made ready to shoot if they did, and rode on till about eighty yards from them, we watching them and they us. Then we went as fast as our horses

could carry us. We got into a motte of trees and brush
and stayed there all night, thinking every noise was
the Indians. In the morning we saw their trail. They
went north, and we found in the road a man whom
they had killed and scalped.

One night some one slipped up to the house of Lynn,
and shot at him through the window. The bullet
barely missed his head. He suspected the man named
Matias, who had hunted with him, and who had said
he would kill him if he got a chance. He thought the
bullet was from that man's gun. Lynn had a dog
which was acquainted with Matias, and that the dog
made no fuss was another reason why he suspected
the man. The dog was a bloodhound. Another reason was that the Mexican woman who raised Lynn
was an aunt of Matias's wife, and Lynn's adopted
mother had in her will given her property to him.
Matias thought his wife should have had part of it.
Lynn always suspected him.

CHAPTER IV.

ON THE LLANO.

I WAS hired to go surveying with a Mr. Montell
to plot land for a German colony on a branch of the
Llano River. There were two parties. Mr. Kelly
had the other. A German boy and I were chainmen
for Mr. Montell. We surveyed tracts twenty-one
miles square. The work was divided between the
two parties. We made a line one mile long and made

a corner, and then at a right angle to the first line
we measured twenty-one miles. Mr. Kelly was to
start from the other end of the mile line and run
across parallel with ours, and meet us at the corner
at the end of the twenty-one-mile course. ·He never
was on time, and laid it on his chainmen.

One Saturday we heard a great roaring sound ahead
of us like the wind. I said it was bees. The men
said it was the wind. At length we came up to a bluff,
and I asked Mr. Montell to let us go and see where
the bees were and get some honey.

"We've no time," said he.

"O yes; let me get some." He finally consented.

The bees were in a hole as big as a barrel in the side
of the bluff, and they poured in and out so thick that
it made a roaring like the wind. The hole was about
twelve feet from the top of the sixty-foot bluff. I told
them to let me down by a rope. The edge of the rock
above the bluff had a round notch the size of a rope
worn in it where the Indians had let men down with
ropes to get honey. They let me down, and I took
my knife from my pocket and cut out a piece of
honey and the bees covered me. I yelled to them to
pull me up quick—that the bees would kill me. They
hauled me up. There was one man, Peacock, who
was awfully afraid of bees, and I took after him. He
yelled at me not to come about him. I said: "I'm
blind; I don't know where I'm going." The bees
stung him and the others, and O he was mad! He
came at me and said: "I'm going to kill you!"

"What are you doing?" the rest said; "don't you
see we are all stung?"

We didn't work on Sunday; and as we camped near, I begged Mr. Montell to let me go and get some more honey. I had left my knife there. A lot of fellows agreed to go with me, but Peacock wouldn't go. I got a lot of old rags and rolled them up, and, when they let me down, I set them afire and stuck them into the hole and went up and waited about half an hour. The bees just poured out, and we got all the honey we could pack away.

Dick Howard, a surveyor, wanted me after this to go with him to survey around Corpus Christi. I went out to the Medina to ask father if I could go. He said that it was too far for a boy to go, and too dangerous. I begged him, but he would not consent. I got on my horse and went anyhow. I was gone three months and got a dollar a day. When I went home, I carried ninety dollars in a belt around my waist. I had spent only two dollars for sugar and coffee. When my father saw me, he said: "Where have you been?"

I said: "I went with Mr. Howard surveying."

"You went without my permission, and I'm going to settle with you; come with me." He cut two long switches and said: "I'm going to wear these out on you. Take off your breeches."

I unbuckled my belt and threw my money down on the ground. It made a great rattling. I was crying, and I said: "Pa, you can whip me if you want to, but it is unjust. If I had been off in idleness, it would be right for you to whip me; but I've been working and I've brought my money home. But I'll tell you now, if you whip me for this, I'll leave here and you'll

2

never see or hear of me again. I'll be like Uncle J—, who went away and has never been heard of since."

"Where did you get that money?" asked my father.

"It's what Mr. Howard paid me for my work, and I've brought it home—more than you and my brothers have cleared in these three months with your teams all together. You can whip me if you want to; but unless you chain me like a dog, you can't keep me at home. I'll go, and you'll never see me again."

"Well, my son, I forgive you," said my father; "and although you are not of age, I set you free. You are your own man from this time; you can go and come at your will."

I gave him the money. He invested it for me in lots in San Antonio, but I never knew it until a short time before he died, when he told me that a certain lot and house were mine, and that he had bought them with that money.

After this I went with Mr. Howard surveying again around Corpus Christi and Capano Bay. Mr. Howard was one of the best men I ever knew. He was a West Pointer, but for some trouble he had there he was expelled and came to the republic of Texas. We got out of rations one day, and went into Corpus Christi. We were buying provisions in a store when a man entered and said to Mr. Howard: "Hello, Dick; what are you doing here?"

"Hello, Whiting; what are *you* doing here? I'm surveying."

"I'm going on a long trip—going to San Antonio to get ready, and then I'm going through to El Paso to see if a road can be opened through the country. Come and go with me, Dick; I'll pay you well."

"Why, I'm surveying here, making money."

"Well, come along with me; I'll give you good wages, and you can see a new country and locate land if you want to. It's a newly opened country."

"Well, what'll you give me?"

"I'll give you three dollars a day and find you."

"Well, if I go, I want this boy to go too" (meaning me).

"What can he do?" asked Whiting.

"Why, he can do more than I can. He can hunt and he can find water. He's my guide; can do most anything in the woods. He would be very useful to us on the trip."

"Well, I'll take him."

"What will you give him?"

"I'll give him two dollars a day."

"Will you go, Polly?"

"I'll go if you do, Dick."

"I'm going."

"Well, I'll go too."

We arranged to meet in San Antonio February 1, 1849, and get ready for the trip. It was now early in the month of January. Mr. W. H. C. Whiting was also a West Pointer, a Virginian, and was a lieutenant in the United States army and an engineer. He afterwards rose to be a general in the Confederate army, and was killed in the War.

CHAPTER V.

WITH THE UNITED STATES ARMY.

AT San Antonio Lieutenant Whiting was joined by
Lieutenant Smith, a topographical engineer. Whiting was in command and Smith assistant. The party
consisted of seventeen, all citizens except the two
lieutenants. There was one Mexican, a mule packer,
Francisco Fuentes, and a Delaware Indian named Jack
Hunter. Early in February the party left San Antonio by way of Fredericksburg. This was a memora-
ble trip. After leaving Fredericksburg we began to
get among the Indians. Signs of them were numer-
ous—trails, camp fires, etc.—but they did not bother us.
We were alarmed one night by a shot, but the sentinel
was mistaken. There was water in abundance until
we left the San Saba; then it failed, and we went
three days without water. Our course lay across
trails which I felt sure led to water. There were
trails of wild horses and of deer, and doves were
seen. All of these I knew must go to water. But Lieutenant Whiting was marching by the compass and
would not change his course; so when the water was
had in our canteens was gone at noon one day, we saw
no more till ten o'clock at night of the third day afterwards. The second day a very light shower fell, and
on our clothes we caught a little water and wet our
mouths. It was very little, but it gave relief. Some
of the men cried for water. It was pitiful. Some
wanted to break off from the party and hunt for water,
but the lieutenant would not allow it. He said to

them: "If you leave us, you will get lost and perish. I must go by my course."

He had his maps and compass, and held us on the course he had decided upon. Five of our pack mules gave out and had to be left. The men who chewed tobacco suffered most. Their tongues were swollen and their mouths were dry. Lieutenant Smith was one of these. The men chewed leaves, bark, and everything that might give them a little relief. I chewed lead to cool my mouth. I had some pinola, which gave me more relief than anything else. Pinola is made of parched corn ground very fine. There is then mixed and ground with it enough sugar to sweeten it, a liberal amount of cinnamon bark, spice, cloves, and a little black pepper. It is all thoroughly ground together again, and makes a very nourishing food. Lieutenant Whiting and I had each about twenty-five pounds. At night of the second day we went into camp, but the neighing of the mules was very pitiful; they would not eat, and the men ate very little. Next day our sufferings increased, and at ten o'clock at night they also ended, for we reached Live Oak Creek, near where Camp Lancaster was afterwards located. We came to the creek where there was a high bank, but the mules and men ran right over it and plunged into the water. The lieutenant called to us that we were in as much danger, now that we had found water, as we were before, if we drank too much. I drank about a quart and stopped; later I drank more. Nobody was hurt by drinking. We were so tired and broken down that we turned the mules loose, and all lay down to sleep. Next day

we traveled but a short distance down the creek and
rested. We then resumed our march, Lieutenant
Whiting holding on his course.

At the mouth of Live Oak Creek we crossed the
Pecos River. The ford was very swift, and we had
great difficulty in getting over. Some of our pack
mules were washed down the stream some distance,
and, the banks being very steep below the ford, we had
to put ropes around the mules and pull them up the
bank. After we got over the Pecos I found and
caught a mare that had been left there a year before by
some party. She was as wild as a deer. We went
up the Pecos River after crossing, and went on to
springs which we named Comanche Springs, because
a large number of Indians of that tribe were camped
there. After leaving this place we camped next night
without water. At this camp I lost my horse. He
was the best and fastest animal I ever had. I called
him Gavilan (hawk). The mare I had caught went
with him. I begged Lieutenant Whiting to let me
go back and hunt my horse. He said he would not
wait for me. There was no water there, but he would
go on to water and wait until I caught up. I went
back by myself on a mare I had caught. I camped by
myself. I killed a deer, and took a ham and head, and
ate the head for my breakfast without salt or bread.
The head of a deer is the best and sweetest part about
him when roasted in the ashes. The next morning
I gave up my horse as lost, and started back to join
our party,* overtaking them at a fine creek where we

---

*The diary of General Whiting, which recently appeared
in the publications of the Southern History Association, con-

rested two days among the Limpio Mountains. The creek was full of fish, and we caught them in great abundance. We were now west of the Pecos and north of the Rio Grande Rivers.

One morning about ten o'clock, as we rose to the summit of a hill, we came suddenly upon an old gray Indian with four or five squaws and a boy. We were right upon them before either party saw the other. The boy ran off into the bushes and stood looking as wild as a scared buck. The squaws stood still, with their mouths open as if struck dumb and paralyzed. We stood looking at them. The old Indian commenced muttering and turning around as if making some incantations. He lifted an old blanket on two ramrods and waved it back and forth, all the time muttering. He then stooped down and gathered handfuls of dust and rubbed it on his breast, talking to the boy who held his little bow and arrows, and to the squaws. He bellowed like a bull. I thought I would speak to him in Spanish, and I said: "Don't be afraid; we will not hurt you."

He replied quickly in good Spanish: "I do not know

---

tains this among other notices of the author: "We had been uneasy for Polly, but to-night he made his appearance. After a long and faithful trailing of the missing animals, he had been forced to give up the search, and we concluded some roving party of Indians had picked them up. This boy Policarpo is one of the most valuable members of my party—a patient and untiring hunter, an unerring trailer, with all the instinct and woodcraft of the Indian combined with the practical part of surveying which he has learned from Howard; moreover, a capital hand with the mules. I don't know of any person whom I would rather have in the woods."

and never knew what fear is. What do you want here? This is our country; what are you here after?"

One of our party, Brady, said in English: "Let's kill that old fool and these old squaws and go on."

"No," said the lieutenant; "we will not hurt them. The old man is making no attempt to hurt us, and we will let them alone. My orders are not to fire first on any Indian."

"Orders? What are orders here in these wilds? I say let's kill them."

"Brady, I obey orders everywhere. These Indians shall not be hurt."

The old Indian, suspecting that his end was near, said (in Spanish): "You can kill us, but you will soon be ground to dust."

"And who'll do it?" said we.

Gathering up a handful of dust and pointing to the mountains, he said: "Those mountains are as full of Indians as my hand of dust, and they'll make dust and powder of you."

"Ah! you can't scare us that way."

"My words go neither that way nor that; they go that way." As he spoke he pointed to the right, then to the left, and then straight before him. He meant that he was telling the truth.

I said to him: "Don't you see we are not after you nor your people? If we were, we would not be mounted on mules but on the fleetest horses. You are not after us, for you are traveling on mules as we are. You are going from one camp to another, just as we are, and we do not mean to harm you."

The old man seemed convinced, and came a little

nearer. His next question was: "Have you got any tobacco?"

"Yes."

"Will you give us some?"

"Yes; come and get it."

He came up, a tall, grizzly old Indian, and we gave him tobacco. The squaws also came up and got tobacco. But one of them had set the prairie on fire. I said: "What does that mean?"

"It is to call the Indians here, and then you'll tell what you are after."

We left them and went on our course, Brady cursing because they were not shot. It was about ten in the morning. About twelve o'clock we saw a great dust rising before us some miles way. Some of the men said: "Look what a drove of antelopes yonder."

After a little I said, "That's not antelopes; it's Indians. Look behind us;" and there behind us came another great drove of Indians. We were in mortal peril. We dismounted and tied our mules together neck to neck, and formed a ring around them and awaited the Indians. Those behind came up first. As they drew near enough to be heard, they began calling to us in Spanish: "No tiren, El capitán viene atrás!"

"Stand off," we said; "don't come up."

They kept calling out: "Don't shoot; the chief is coming, and wants to talk to you."

In the meantime they were dividing out and forming a ring around us, but keeping out of range. In a short time the chief came up. It was Chino Huero (Blonde Curls, so called because his hair was light and inclined to curl). He proved to be the son of the old Indian we had met in the morning. One of the squaws was his wife, and the boy was his son. We had passed them without harming them, had shown kindness to them when they were in our power, and this chief appreciated it. Very soon the party in front of us also came up. There must have been three hundred of them. They halted and the chiefs came forward. Chino Huero was busy talking to his men, evidently explaining something to them. Among those who came up with the party from before was one man mounted on a beautiful horse with a Mexican saddle and bridle. He wore a Mexican sombrero and a short jacket, and looked like a Mexican, except he was very dark. His only weapon was a long, slender lance which he rested on the ground. He stood apart from the rest, taking no part in the conversation. Those who were calling to us did not speak Spanish distinctly, and I, thinking the silent man could speak Spanish, called to them and asked that they get that man (pointing to him) to interpret for them. He spoke up sternly in good Spanish: "I am interpreter for nobody."

There was in our party a man who understood the Indian dialect and knew this man, and he said to me: "That is Gomez, the head chief, and you have almost insulted him."

Chino Huero exerted himself to keep his men back from us. They were eager to press on us and finish us in short order. We stood with our arms ready, watching every movement and awaiting the issue of their parley. At length Gomez, whose air was menacing and whose few movements were hostile, called out: "This is no place to talk; these men must go to my camp."

I did the interpreting, and I said to the lieutenant: "Gomez says we must go to his camp." I added: "If we do, they will kill us. He wants to get us away from here and kill us."

The lieutenant answered: "We will not go; let us do our talking here."

I translated it for Gomez.

"Not go? We'll make you go; we'll drag you there!" said Gomez, and the words shot from him like an arrow. His whole bearing changed instantly; his eyes flashed, and he wheeled toward his men and in Indian dialect began to issue his commands. They rushed forward and formed a circle around us outside of Chino Huero's men. Then another circle outside of that was formed, and we were surrounded by three circles of Indians, every one eager to pounce upon us. The Indians all dismounted from their ponies, some of them stripped themselves almost naked, and were pressing upon us. Some were piling up the rocks before them to shoot from. Chino Huero rushed forward to Gomez and began talking very energetically and earnestly. He looked as if pleading a case with the greatest earnestness. He was repeating the story of our meeting his father in the morning and sparing the whole party when they were all in our power. He declared his purpose to defend those who had spared his father, his wife, and child. He told Gomez he had always been his friend, but if he harmed these people their friendship would not only end, but he would have to pass over his dead body and those of his men to reach his victims. He paused, but Gomez appeared morose and unmoved. Chino Huero began again. The spirit and energy of his every movement were most admirable. He was tall and lithe, and he pleaded his cause with skill and great force. At last he so far succeeded that Gomez ordered a council of all the chiefs. Three or four other chiefs came forward. They took the goatskins off their saddles and spread them on the ground together. They then retired a little way and took off their moccasins, walked barefoot to their places, seated themselves in a ring, faces inward, and began their deliberations. Lieutenant Whiting, Dick Howard, and I were taken into the council. They lighted a pipe and passed it. It cannot easily be imagined what were our feelings as that powwow progressed. I had myself resolved what I would do. When I first saw our peril it seemed as if all the blood had left my body; my feelings were very strange. It seemed at first as if I were being lifted from the ground. I recollect I raised my heart to God and said: "My last day is come; God help me to die like a brave man." Then I was fully resolved and felt that I did not care whether I died or not, I was going to do some desperate fighting. I stood there waiting and picking out my men. I had fully resolved to kill Gomez the first man. The council ended. The eloquence and inflexible purpose of Chino Huero won even against the head chief. Gomez directed him to tell the men. He sprang to his pony and rode three times very rapidly around the ring, talking all the time rapidly to his men. Then he went round twice more much more slowly and talking much more deliberately. Then he came forward and told us the chief had decided to spare us and let us go, on condition that we should not disturb them. They wanted to remain in that country, even if it was barren. It would be of no use to us, but they could live on grass and roots. The Indians were evidently still displeased and kept watching us and pressing upon us, so that the chiefs could with difficulty keep them back. We asked them to let us go, but Gomez said: "No; you have nothing to eat, and must go to my camp."

We asked him to keep his men back from us. They wanted only to see, he said, and would not hurt us. But they were hostile and threatening in their movements. Finally it was agreed that we would go to the camp of Gomez, but we insisted that they must all go before us and show us the way, and we would follow. We feared treachery if they came in our rear. They agreed and moved on before. In a short time about sixty of them—young fellows—began holding back and dropping along our sides and working to the rear. We stopped still and let them go on. In a little while Gomez came galloping back to us and asking why we had stopped. We explained that he must keep his men in front as he had agreed.

"They won't hurt you," he declared, but ordered them on, and then we moved on. We were sure those young bucks meant to get in our rear and take us with their lances. Fortunately five antelopes came running out and attracted the attention of these young fellows, and they started after them and killed three

of the five. We reached the camp and tied our mules.
This camp was by a little spring which came from
under the mountain. There must have been four hundred Indians in the camp. They had their wigwams
pitched, scattered around without order, near the
water. These wigwams were made by tying a number of slender poles together at the top, spreading out
the lower ends and covering them with hides of deer,
buffalo, or other wild animals. The squaws, the children, and many of the men crowded around and
pressed upon us. We were thus huddled together,
and could hardly turn around. We asked that the
people be kept away.

"O, they'll not hurt you; they just want to see you,"
was the answer. We did not feel safe, and they greatly annoyed us. We found it necessary to make ar-
rangements to get something to eat. We saw some
cows come up to water, and asked whose they were.
They were Gomez's, and he agreed to sell us one, but
did not want money; he wanted powder and lead.
We told him we could not trade that way. He then
agreed to take three blankets for the cow, and picked
out the lieutenant's blanket, Collin's, and mine. The
lieutenant had paid twenty-five dollars for his and I
sixteen for mine. The lieutenant said he would not
sell his blanket for ten cows. Gomez then agreed to
take two blankets—Collin's and mine. Lieutenant
Whiting said that he would pay me what I gave for
mine. It was getting along in February; and as I had
two, I let mine go. I tied the cow down so she could
not get up, and decided to leave her until morning
before we killed her. We lay down at night, but we

did not sleep. We could hear them still arguing our case during the night and quarreling among themselves. Those Indians kept crawling up to us and looking at us all through the night. It was not a pleasant sight to see a shaggy head and a dark face raised a little above the ground peering at one in the dark. They meant us evil, and only sought their opportunity.

Next morning we killed the cow, and it was decided that we should accompany Chino Huero to his camp. (He and his men had stayed with us.) When we got there, he asked us to stay two days and rest, and the lieutenant consented. In those two days we ate up our cow, and had arranged to start the next morning for Presidio del Norte. Chino Huero agreed to send with us an Indian to show us the trail to Presidio del Norte if we would pay the Indian something. He agreed to go with us for a blanket, and selected mine. He was mounted on a wild bronco, and in the morning of the first day his horse broke with him and ran off to the right and kept on out of sight. We said, "He's gone; we'll not see him again," but after a while he came back. He did that three times, and each time we were sure he was gone; but again he returned and led us to the trail. We could kill nothing to eat the first and second days. Jack Hunter was busy, but brought nothing in. The lieutenant had a little pinola, and he gave us a teaspoonful each three times a day. When we were nearly starved, I begged the lieutenant to let me go out hunting. I went and took Jack. We agreed where we would meet the command in the evening. I went outside of a little

hill, far off to the right of the course, and told Jack
to take the other side. If he heard me fire, he was to
come to me; if he fired, I would go to him. I had not
gone far into the woods before I saw a big black wild
buck and shot him. Jack came, and we put the deer
on our mules and started to camp. On the way I
shot a jack rabbit and a prairie dog.

When we got in sight of our men, they began hallooing and throwing up their hats. They asked who
killed the deer, and when I said "I did," they hugged
me and lifted me off the ground and hurrahed to
their hearts' content. We seventeen hungry men ate
every particle of that deer, rabbit, and prairie dog for
our supper. We had observed Indians following us off
on the mountain side; so we built large fires and packed
our mules, left the fires burning and traveled all
night and all next day, and in the evening reached
Presidio del Norte.

We rested a few days at Presidio del Norte with
Ben Lytton, for whom Fort Lytton is named. We
had some fun at Lytton's expense. By some means
we got a bundle of newspapers in the camp and they
were divided out among us. Lytton had one. We
were all seated reading; somebody nudged me and
motioned to Lytton. He was holding his paper up-
side down. The men could not hold in. It was clear
that Lytton could not read, though he was a man of
excellent sense and supplied us with everything we
needed.

From Presidio del Norte to El Paso there was
nothing of special interest. We saw several parties
of Indians, but they passed like a flash and did not

disturb us. We saw signs of silver ore, quartz rock
abounded, and mines have since been developed there.
At Presidio del Norte we were joined by two more
men, and at El Paso by several, one of whom (Skillman) was a noted Indian fighter. Our number had
increased to twenty-five when we were ready for the
return march. We camped at El Paso, then called
Coon's Ranch, opposite Paso del Norte (now known
as Ciudad Juarez). Coon had a ranch, a store, and a
train of mules that traded to Santa Fe, and went
sometimes as far as St. Louis. We bought supplies
from him and from the Mexican families.*

CHAPTER VI.

BACK FROM EL PASO.

ON our return from El Paso we followed the Rio
Grande River until we found trails coming into the
river from the mountains. We followed these, knowing, as they led through a gap in the mountain, we
should find water. We passed through dense pine
forests and an immense prairie dog town miles and
miles in extent. I hunted on the return trip. I had
one of the best mules I ever saw. He could trail like
a dog. He would put his nose to the ground and
strike a trail and follow it in the night as well as in

---

*See also the Whiting Diary for an account of the exciting
episode with Chino Huero and Gomez.—ED.

the day. I kept the party in meat. I killed more meat than Jack Hunter did. One day we started a brown cinnamon bear, the first one I ever saw. I ran him for eight or ten miles, but he got away from me. When we reached the Pecos River, we rested one day to fish. Fish were very abundant, and we feasted on them. This is a swift, narrow, dangerous river with high, steep banks. We came near being drowned. Near the Ojo Escondido a party of sixty or seventy Indians came near as if they were going to attack us. They were Lipans. We were in the bed of a little creek, and they were afraid to attack us and left us.

One day one of the men said: "Look ahead; there are two Indians."

"No," I said; "they are not Indians, they are Spanish daggers; don't you see them running? Stop your mules and you will see they will stop." So they did.

Our rations ran short; we had nothing but meat— venison. Skillman and two others were sent forward to Fort Inge to get rations. They took my mule. I was so attached to him I almost cried. He was so kind and gentle and smart. The first night out the Indians stole him and all the mules of the Skillman party. They went on afoot, but reached the fort only a little before we did. The trip was useless; and had it not been made, we would not have lost our mules. Men who are sent ahead for special service should not go into camp, but go right ahead to the end of the trip.

Fort Inge was a noted place in the early days. It was situated by a solitary round hill which rose out of the plain, and was a landmark for all the country. The Leona Creek rises there. The place took its

name from an officer of the army. At the time we
passed the United States Second Dragoons was
camped there under the command of General Hardee.
We remained two or three days, and went on toward
San Antonio and came to the Leon Creek, eight miles
from the town, and met a man who told us that the
cholera was bad in San Antonio. The lieutenant decided to take a vote as to whether we should go into
the stricken town. He said he would not vote, but
formed us into a line and asked all who were in favor
of going on to step one step forward, and if the
majority were in favor of entering they would go on.
I wanted to go on. I was, shame to tell, covered
with body lice, and all the rest were in the same fix.
I felt I must go and get some clean clothes. I had
thrown away one suit, but the one I wore was infested.
The majority voted to go in, and we all proceeded.
Some were great drinkers and they wanted liquor.
Jack Hunter was thirsty, and so was Brady. Nearly
all the men got drunk when we reached town. On the
trip we had had no liquor, and it was a good thing;
liquor would have been the ruin of us.

The lieutenant paid us off and disbanded us, but
before he did so he gave me a fine recommendation to
Major Belga, the quartermaster at the post. He said:
"Major, I have one favor to ask of you before we part.
I find letters here calling me home, but I want to rec-
ommend this boy to you [meaning me]. I want you
to keep him in the service, whether you have anything
for him to do or not. He is a very useful boy. He
can do anything a man can. He can be guide, boss
packer, boss teamster, hunter, interpreter, or any-

thing you like. I may come back and I may not; but
I want you to keep him."

"Well, Whiting, I'll do it. What do you pay him?"

"Sixty dollars a month."

"I can't pay him that much, but I'll give him at
least forty-five and rations."

"Will you stay for that, Polly?"

"Yes, I'll stay," and I stayed ten months, getting
forty-five dollars per month for doing almost nothing.

Before he left, Lieutenant Whiting said to me:
"Polly, I want to see your father before I go; is he
here?"

"No; but he is coming to-morrow."

"Well, bring him in to see me."

The next day I took father to see him, and I said:
"Lieutenant, this is my father."

He asked me if he spoke English.

I said: "Not a word."

But the lieutenant spoke Spanish. He asked father how many sons he had.

"Ten," he said.

"Well, I don't know your others, but I know you
haven't got another like this one."

"No; I haven't."

He told father how I had hunted, and said I'd kept
them alive on the trip; that I'd leave them in the
morning when every man was afraid to leave the
command, be gone all day, and come back at night
loaded with venison and game. Father was frightened
by the things he told him of the trip, and said he
could not let me go again.

"O," I said, "I've promised to go and help open

the road the lieutenant has located, and I shall have to go when the time comes."

We got back to San Antonio about the last of April, having spent about three months in making the trip.

CHAPTER VII.

WITH WAGONS ON THE PLAINS.

IN June, 1849, Colonel Joseph E. Johnston arrived at San Antonio to open the road to El Paso which Lieutenant Whiting had located. Dick Howard was employed as first guide and I as second. A large number of laborers were employed, and a regiment of troops, the Third United States Infantry, accompanied us. A large wagon train went with supplies of all kinds. Colonel Johnston called me and said: "Polly, I will employ you for this trip, but you must promise me that you will not leave me."

. He had got a hint that I wanted to go to California, and I did want to go; it was during the gold excitement; so I studied about it some time. At last I told him I would not leave him, and he employed me at sixty dollars a month. Colonel Joseph E. Johnston was one of the finest men I ever knew. He was very quiet; the quietest man, I think, I ever knew.

I had a great deal to do. I would go ahead to find the marks of our survey, and then come back to guide the teams. Where the prairie was smooth and open the colonel gave the teamsters orders to follow me and not turn to the right or left; and I led them in a perfectly straight line. When you looked back from the front, you could see but one wagon— the one in front. The road we made was beautiful. You could see the white trail through the clay soil for miles and miles as straight as an arrow. The troops followed on behind us. We went by all the springs that lay along the course. Game of every kind was abundant, and we lived on the fat of the land. I would go ahead one week and Dick Howard the next; but often he would have something else to do, and I did most of that work. The men used to beg me to take them with me. They wanted to hunt. I did not like a large party, but sometimes took one or two at a time. There was a lawyer from San Antonio named Edwards along with us just for the trip. He used to go with me. He was a fine man and was one of my best friends, and used to say to me: "Polly, anything in the world I can do for you, just ask me."

When we reached El Paso, Colonel Johnston detailed a party to go across to the Pecos and see if a road could be made through a gap in the mountains. Lieutenant Smith was in charge, and I was along. While on this trip we saw a horse and two or three people about two miles ahead of us. I said: "Lieutenant, yonder is that horse that was stolen from one of our men."

"Do you think you can tell a horse two miles off, Polly?"

"Yes, sir; that is the horse. I know that horse." It was a very notable animal, coal-black with a large white ring in his face as round as if made by a compass.

"Well, if you think so, go after it; and if it is ours, bring all the party. How many men do you want?"

"Two."

I picked out two, and we loped off and came up to them. There were two men and a woman (Mexicans). They had on the horses a large rawhide and a sack filled with dried meat. They had stolen a beef and killed it, and were making their way to the Apache Indians. When we told them they must go back with us, the woman began to cry.

I said: "Don't cry; we're not going to hurt you."

We took them to the company, and Lieutenant Smith, after questioning them about the theft, turned the men over to the guard. They thought we were going to kill them. The woman began crying. We told her she would not be hurt. She begged us to take her with us; said the men had stolen her, telling her they would take her to California. They had deceived her and brought her here, and she did not know where she was. We agreed to take her back to El Paso.

Next morning Lieutenant Smith said to me: "Polly, I'm going to give you a job—you and two men. Stay here with these fellows; and when we're gone some distance, get you good switches and switch them good and let them go."

When the party was nearly out of sight, I said to the thieves: "Well, my friends, I'm left here for a very serious business. [Then they thought we were about to kill them.] But before I attend to it, I'm going to talk to you some."

I told them they had to promise me that if I let them

off they would not steal anything as long as they lived,
nor deceive anybody as they had the woman Paula.
They said they would promise whatever I wanted
them to. I made them promise in the presence of
God and the men that they would behave themselves
the balance of their days, and then I let them go. I
did not whip them. The woman went back to El
Paso with us. She was a peon; and when the command was ready to return, she begged us to let her,
go to San Antonio with us. I said that I would have
to ask the colonel. I went to him and made the re-
quest. He was a jocular man, and said: "Not unless
you marry her, Polly."

"O, I can't do that," I said, and I was leaving when
he called me back and said: "Can she be of any use
to you, Polly?"

"Yes, sir; she can cook and wash for our mess, and
can wash for others too."

"Well, she can go. You can let her ride in any
of the wagons she wants to."

The man who had her in peonage at El Paso heard
she was with us, and came up one day making inquiry
for her. He was told that she was there, but that
he could not get her. He went to Colonel Johnston
and handed him a document. The colonel called me
when he had read it, and said: "This man wants that
woman. Let everything stop; we must settle this
matter. Call the woman."

She came, looking as pale as death.

"Ask her if she knows this man," said the colonel.

"Yes, sir; she says she knows him."

"How long has she known him?"

"For eighteen or twenty years."

"What has she been doing for him?"

"Cooking."

"What has he paid her?"

"About a dollar and a half a month. He says she owes him about seventy dollars."

"What is the debt for?"

"She says for funeral expenses for her mother; that she went to this man to pay the debt by personal service."

The colonel asked the man: "How is it that she has not paid that debt in all that time?"

"Because she took up more all the time than her wages came to."

"Ask her, Polly," said the colonel, "if she wants to go back with this man."

"No, sir; she does not."

"Then she can go on with us, as she is free, or go back, as she pleases. I can't send any of my men back to take her. You can go, sir," he said to the man, and he went back.

The woman went on to San Antonio. She made thirty dollars a month washing for one company, and another group paid her five a month for cooking. She had sixty or seventy dollars when she got to San Antonio.

On this trip Colonel Johnston took a party and went down the Pecos to see if the road could not be made from Beaver Lake to the Neuces and greatly shorten the distance from San Antonio to El Paso. Leaving Beaver Lake, we traveled through a very rough country and marched one day and camped without water.

Next morning as we were going along I saw a tremendous black bear ahead of us. I said: "Colonel, let me go and kill that bear; we are out of meat."

"Whom do you want to go with you?"

"Two men, so if I miss they can shoot it."

We galloped on ahead. The bear went into a little thicket. One of the mules brayed, and I bounded off my mule, to the astonishment of the men. I knew the bear had not scented us, and as soon as it heard the mule it would be apt to stand up on his hind feet to see what it was. Sure enough it reared up—a tremendous big she-bear, rolling fat. I leveled my gun and shot it right in the sticking place. The men came up and we cut the bear up, hide and all, every man taking a piece of meat and of fat. That night we were all very tired and thirsty, and we did not get up next morning till about sunup. When I picked up my blanket, I said: "Come here, boys, and look what I slept on."

There lay a big rattlesnake coiled up. I had slept on him all night, and he was mashed nearly flat. I killed him.

We reached San Antonio in October, 1849, and every man was discharged from the service except me. I was retained at a salary of forty-five dollars a month, and I continued in the service for twelve years, or up to 1861, the beginning of the War.

CHAPTER VIII.

A PANTHER STORY.

I REMAINED in the employ of Major Belga, quarter-master, and was sent out as guide with scouting parties of mounted infantry looking after Indians; but the soldiers were not practiced riders, and we were not successful. In the winter of 1850 the officers decided to take a bear hunt, and I went with them. I got a pack of splendid hounds from a friend, and we went about nine miles from San Antonio to the Potranca Creek. I had a splendid horse and could keep up with the hounds. We started a bear the first day—an immense fellow—and I killed it. We started a panther, and I killed that. Next day the dogs treed another panther. The tree was on the edge of a bluff. I was down below under the bluff, and the officers were above. I was about to shoot, when they called out: "Don't you shoot, Polly; you kill everything. We are going to kill that panther."

I said: "I can shoot it in the head and kill it dead from where I am."

"Don't you do it; you hold on."

"If you shoot from where you are," I replied, "you'll only wound it, and it will drop down and kill our dogs and end our hunt."

"Never mind," they said.

I was mad, for I expected some of the dogs to get torn to pieces. They fired away, and the panther dropped to the ground. The dogs sprang onto it, and such fighting you never saw. The panther threw them right and left, and cut some of them badly. It made its way down the side of the bluff to its den, with the dogs after it. It went into a sort of cave, and I felt sure some of the dogs would be killed, and I started after it into the den. The officers called after me not to go, but to let the dogs go.

"Don't you go in there if every dog gets killed."

But I was angry. I climbed up to the mouth of the den and pulled the dogs away by their tails and threw them down the bluff out of my way. All the dogs were there but one. Then I went into the cave. It was so dark I couldn't see, but I could hear a choking noise as if the dog and panther were clinched. I felt around for them, and got hold of the dog's tail and dragged them both to the light clinched together. The dog had the panther by the throat, and the panther the dog by the neck. I put my pistol to the panther's head and shot him dead. He let go his hold and limbered out, and I dragged him out of the den by the tail. The officers were hallooing and calling out to know what I had done, if I had killed him; and saying they wouldn't have gone in there for all the dogs and money in the country. On that hunt we killed nine bears, three panthers, twelve turkeys, and any number of smaller game. We had a fine time; everybody enjoyed it. Lieutenant Dodge, one of the party, was the tallest man I ever saw. He must have been six feet eight inches. He was an infantry officer, but made a good hunter. It was the first hunt for many of the young officers.

When we returned, we were ordered out on a scout after Indians, with Lieutenant Barbour in charge.

The night after we started there fell a very heavy rain, and we lost the trail of the Indians. I was going ahead when I saw in the distance seven buffaloes, the first I had ever seen. I rode back and motioned to the lieutenant to stop the men and told him I had seen seven animals, the strangest I ever saw. I thought they must be buffalo. I said: "Let's take two or three men and go ahead and kill one or two of them."

He called to the sergeant to order two or three men who could ride and run well. I was watching the buffalo. They started, and I yelled, "The buffalo are gone; let's all charge them!" and away we went pellmell, the whole company, pack mules and all, charging the buffalo. My horse got scared. A horse is awfully afraid of a buffalo; the smell is so bad and the shape is ugly. A horse hates them. My horse broke with me and stampeded. He turned and ran, snorting and plunging; all I could do to keep him from breaking. The whole company got stampeded, and away they went in every direction. Some men lost their guns, their caps, and pistols. I brought my horse around in a wide circle by spurring, whipping, and talking to him, and came up with a cow and shot at her. I was about to shoot again with the pistol when she fell over and I went on. The lieutenant was with me. I looked back and the cow was getting up. I was making for her, and the lieutenant said: "Let me get a shot."

He fired, and his horse commenced to buck and threw him. I called to him to hold on to his bridle rein: if the horse got away, we'd never catch him. He held on, and the horse dragged him all around, the

buffalo cow trying meantime to get at him, but he
held to his horse.   We killed the cow, and spent all the
evening hunting up the lost hats and guns, etc.   Some
of them we never found, and the men went bareheaded.
We camped near, and the next day went back to San
Antonio.

I went about 1851 with a Mr. McDonell to the
San Saba to survey.   While engaged in the work, a
party of ten or twelve Indians came near us, and a
Mexican woman came into our camp and asked if I
were not a Mexican.   When she found that I was,
she begged me to let her go with us.   She was Chief
Yellow Wolf's wife, and he had two others.   I asked
Mr. McDonell; but he said it was very dangerous,
that we were so few in numbers.   She cried and
begged us; but we told her it was impossible, we
could not take her.   They hung around our camp.
Mr. McDonell suspected them, but they said they
wanted to trade.   I traded my blanket for a fine buffalo robe.   Still they hung around us and looked sus-
picious.   Yellow Wolf wanted to know why we were
taking their lands.   McDonell determined to leave.
We told them we were going to another place.   We
traveled all night and all next day, and saw no more
of them.   McDonell agreed to pay me two dollars a
day, but he paid me only one.   He wanted me to
go with him again later, but I refused.   I would
never have anything more to do with him.

CHAPTER IX.

COWARDS AND TRAITORS.

In the winter of 1851 Major Belga ordered me to go as guide with Colonel McCall, Inspector General, to El Paso. The trip to El Paso was without incident of importance. Colonel McCall went on from El Paso to New Mexico, and I was left without anybody to return to San Antonio with me. The colonel told me I should have to go alone, or wait till some opportunity presented itself for company. If I could have had one man, I would have gone back, but I would not start alone. I was in the meantime offered the place of assistant wagon master to go with a train of ninety wagons to Socorro, N. Mex. I accepted the offer and went. Those teamsters were a wild set of men. The wagon master was of the same kind. Gambling was their chief business when not traveling. Once we suffered greatly for water, going a day and a half without it. We had in the party a Frenchman, who was a great braggart, always telling what he could and would do if we got among Indians. He was always at it. All the time it was swagger and brag and blow. I got tired of it. I told the wagon master that fellow was a coward, and I was going to have some fun at his expense if he would allow me. He was in for it, and I asked him to let me set the guard that night. I put this fellow on guard, and put him on the outside post. I loaded his pistols for him without balls. I said to him: "I'll give you two pistols, as you are on the outpost. Be on the lookout; and if there are any Indians about, be sure to do something."

I went back and disguised myself like an Indian. I tied a handkerchief around my head and put a blanket around me. I fixed up another man in the same way, and I said: "Now, we will go out beyond that fellow and I'll call like an owl and you'll answer me, and we will come toward each other, and when we get up pretty close we'll rush at him. I'll shoot, and we'll run him into camp."

The moon was shining. We left all the camp playing cards, and went out beyond our man. We hooted dolefully like owls, and answered each other, and crept nearer and nearer. I made right for him at last, and he saw me. I fired and kept running at him, yelling like a wild Indian. I expected him to shoot at me with his pistols, but he did not stop even to aim at me; he broke and ran, and I after him. He was looking back at me and ran square against a tree and knocked himself down. I kept yelling and shooting around him. He was scared almost to death. He picked himself up and went yelling into camp, and alarmed everybody by bellowing that he saw eight or ten Indians after him. It broke up gambling for the balance of that night; but the Indians did not come, and the wagon master did not seem alarmed by his story. The man who went with me let the story out, and we never heard any more bragging from that Frenchman. He was unmercifully ridiculed, but he was taught a good lesson.

When I got back to El Paso, Lieutenant Mecklin was about to start to San Antonio on a furlough.

There were in his party a number of discharged soldiers whose time had expired, and a number of others like himself going home on leave. I joined this party. We were coming down the Rio Grande, and were about opposite the town of Guadalupe in camp at noon, when one of the enlisted soldiers deserted and swam the river to the Mexican side. When he got across, he stood on the bank and cursed the officers and insulted and abused everybody in the whole party. The lieutenant said to me: "Polly, I want you to go and get that man and bring him back dead or alive. Will you do it?"

"Yes, sir; I'll do it.

"How many men do you want?"

"Just one man," I said.

I took a man named Culberson, and we swam the river on our horses. Culberson got out and went up the bank, but I could not make my horse go out of the water and climb the bank. In spite of all I could do, he turned back into the river and started across. I could not control him by anything I could do. He swam out into the stream with me, and got into a sucking eddy. The current was very strong and drew him under, and I saw that both of us were about to be drowned. I slipped off my horse, intending to take hold of his tail and, with his load thus lightened, let him swim out and pull me out with him. I held my gun up in one hand to keep it dry, but as I slipped off the strong current dashed me away from my horse and I could not take hold of his tail. I swam with one hand, holding up my gun with the other. I had on my pistol and my shot pouch with

4

more than two hundred bullets in it. I struggled
against the power of the current with all my might.
I am a good swimmer, but I could make no headway
against that awful suck. I was being drawn down.
To drop my gun was almost like drowning to me—
my gun that Lynn had made and given me. If I
held on to it, I was sure I would drown. I dropped
it. It was like dropping my heart. Strange I never
thought to unbuckle my belt and let my pistol drop
off, or to throw off my shot pouch. With both hands
I then battled with the water for life. My strength
was failing; I could hardly keep my head up. The
water rose to my chin. I felt my head sinking. My
nose went under and I sank. I was drowning. I
struck the bottom. I had strength to catch at the
rocks and roll and crawl along. I got hold of a root
and grasped it and followed it, dragging myself along,
feeling as if I were going to sleep. There was no
sense of pain. I pulled myself along by that last hope,
and got hold of a long mesquite root and finally
dragged myself, nearer dead than alive, to the bank.
That root that saved me was from a mesquite tree
that stood on the high bank where the current had
cut the earth away and left its long root sticking out
into the water—a tree that throws out the longest
roots of any tree I know except the cypress. Culberson saw all my struggles in the water with amazed
looks. When I sank, he thought I was gone; and
when I pulled out by that root, he called to me that
he thought I was drowned. I lay there panting and
resting, unable to get up. I heard my horse above
me trying to get up the bank. When he heard my

voice replying to Culberson, he came down the bank toward me; and when near me, I called to him to stop and he stood still till I could get up. Culberson swam back farther up the river. He had a splendid horse; and when he came to me, I mounted, and we went on and overtook the command, I feeling that I had been drowned; and I had passed through the experience, except the last unconscious stage.

The second night after this experience, Culberson, a German named Klein, and another man named Sam Moon were put on guard. They all deserted and crossed into Mexico. One of them stole my horse—Culberson, I think. Klein had quite a sum of money. As was learned afterwards, Culberson and the other man, Moon, robbed and killed Klein, and for some years those men operated up and down the river as robbers and desperadoes. Both were at last killed at El Paso when resisting arrest. My reflection on the desertion of Culberson was, that if my horse had gone up the bank that day Culberson would have joined the deserter, turned against me, and killed me. Such, I believe, would have been my end.

I was so distressed by the loss of my gun that Lieutenant Mecklin told me to look through the detachment, and if I found a gun that suited me, he would buy it for me. I found a very old gun that suited me, and he bought it for me. My old friend, Jacob Lynn, made a new gun out of it for me. He bored it out larger, rifled it, and restocked it. It proved to be as good as the one I lost in the river.

CHAPTER X.

THE RIGHT YOUNG LADY.

AFTER returning to San Antonio, Major Belga sent me with a train of wagons of corn to Forts Ewell and Merrill, on the Nueces. The Nueces was very high from the rains, and we made a raft of logs and ferried the wagons over, one at a time. The corn was delivered, and I started to return. An escort of a few soldiers was with us. One day we were approached by a party of Indians. They stood off at some distance and said they wanted to trade. I told the spokesman we were not trading, and for them to keep off, to come no nearer. Still they insisted on trading, and when told again and again that we were not traders, one of them wanted me to come out and talk. I said: "You separate from your crowd and come out, and I'll meet you."

He came out and insisted that they were friendly, and wanted to talk with us. I told him to go on his way; if he was friendly and did not want to fight, neither did we. Finally they moved on. As soon as they were out of sight I sent two soldiers back to Fort Ewell to tell the commander of the Indians, and that they could now have an opportunity to gratify their wish to encounter Indians. That message got me into trouble later on. The commander sent out a detachment with a guide to pursue the Indians, but they failed, very strangely, to find the trail, and went back to the fort believing they had been deceived. After I got to San Antonio, Major Belga called me

and showed me a letter from the commander of
Fort Ewell, in which he accused me of having caused
troops to be sent out on a false alarm, for which I
was responsible, and of having brought a keg of liquor into the camp and sold it to the men, and order-
ing Major Belga to discharge me. The Major said:
"Polly, if you can't fix this up, I shall have to obey
orders and discharge you; but I want you to go and
fix this up if you can."

I assured him I could fix it up, and told him I would
go at once and do it. I went alone, dangerous as it
was, all the way back to Fort Ewell, and presented
myself to the commander and told him my business,
and in disproof of the charge of raising a false alarm,
I asked him to call the soldiers I had sent back and
question them. This he did, and they both testified
to having seen the Indians. I told him that a number of other men would testify to the same, and that
all the teamsters could be called, if necessary, and
would testify to having seen the Indians. The commander was satisfied of my innocence of that charge.
As to the other, that of selling liquor to the men, I said
that I did not believe any man would face me and
say that I sold liquor to the soldiers. He called a
man and asked him if he had not said that I sold
liquor to the soldiers.

"I was told so," he replied.

"By whom?"

He named the man. He was sent for, and said he
had been told that I did it. And so on it went. The
author of the rumor could not be located. The commander then directed that a letter be written to Major

Belga saying that I had been acquitted of all the charges. I went back with the document; and when I showed it to Major Belga, he was much pleased and said: "I knew it would be that way."

Returning from this trip, I swam my horse across the Frio River, which was at the time very high. The weather was cold, and I nearly froze. I was wet above my waist, but my matches were dry. I rode up to a large Spanish dagger (yucca), which was covered with dry, dead bark and leaves. I stuck a match to it, and it burned like tinder. I warmed by it, as did my horse also.

I was very soon after this sent with another train, this time of carts loaded also with corn. On this trip, I came very near being killed. One of my cousins got behind with his carts. I was vexed with him for not keeping up, and started back to him. I thought I would disguise myself as an Indian and scare him. As I rode up the others with him ran off, but he did not run. He got his shotgun and took deliberate aim at me, and it was my turn to be scared. It took all the begging I could do to keep him from firing. When I convinced him who I was, he trembled like a leaf, so near he was to killing me. I resolved then never to try to scare another man.

About this time my father came to me one day and said: "Son, I hear you are going to get married."

"No," I said; "I am not."

"Why, a man that claims to know tells me so; says you are engaged to Miss ——."

"No, father, I am not. When I am ready to marry, I will not deny it; I will tell you."

He gave me excellent advice about the kind of girl I should marry. He said that the girl he thought I had in mind would not suit me; she was not domestic; she had money, and would always want to control me in business and financial matters.

I had intended to marry when I returned from El Paso; but when I arrived and found the cholera epidemic in the town, great was my sorrow to find that my beautiful Jesusita was dead. The cholera had robbed me of my promised wife. Twice again I made up my mind to marry, and each time the young lady died. Three times death robbed me of my intended, and I said: "I am not to marry."

But afterwards I did what was a strange thing for me in those days: I prayed. I asked God to show me the one I should marry. There was a young lady of my acquaintance, but whom I had never thought of marrying. One day I was returning from a hunt, and I saw her and another on the walls of the old Alamo building. They called to me to know where I had been, and asked me to come up to them. I had some flowers in my hand. One of them asked me for the flowers, but I said: "No; I didn't get them for you."

"O please give them to me."

"I'll give you some of them."

"And I'll call you my flower," she said.

"No; I don't want you to call me that."

I handed the rest of the flowers to the other young lady, who had not spoken all the time. Afterwards I went to her mother's house, and when I went in I found her alone sewing. In an instant I recalled my prayer, and I said: "This is the one." Before I left

I asked her how she thought we could get along together.

She said: "I think we could get on very well."

"If you do, and will agree to it, we will get married sixty days from now."

She agreed.

"But," I said, "what about your mother?" (Her father was dead.)

"She will agree, because once when I wanted to marry she told me if I would not marry that young man I might marry anybody I pleased, even if he were a colored man. Now, I will hold her to her promise, and she cannot object."

"Very well," I said; "then we will be married in sixty days." She agreed.

I told my father and took him to see her. I was gone for a few weeks. When I came back I said: "What do you think of her, father?"

"My son, you could not find a better girl in all the country."

I told the quartermaster I wanted him to give me a little furlough, that I was going to be married.

"How much do you want?" he asked.

"Fifteen days," I said.

"All right; you can have it."

My father asked me not to have a feast and frolic, but said that a quiet wedding at the young lady's home was best. I agreed. I went to see the bishop about marrying me. He said: "I am told you are a Mason."

"I am," I said.

"You will have to confess."

"I can do that, but I will not confess the secrets of Masonry."

"I don't want that. I know more about Masonry than you do. I will marry you as a Protestant and your wife as a Catholic."

"All right," I said; "but if you do not want to marry me, you can send a priest to the house to do it. If you cannot do that, I can get the justice to marry me for five dollars."

"I'll send a priest," he said.

The evening of my wedding was rainy, and when I sent for the priest he would not come. I took a horse and went after him. He said: "It is raining, and I won't go."

"I've got a horse for you."

"But I can't ride a horse," he said.

"I'll lead the horse," I said, "and here are a gum coat and pants to keep you dry."

He wanted me to pay him more for going with me. I got him on the horse and led the horse through the streets to the house. It was dark. When he had married me, I said: "What do I owe you?"

"Whatever you have a mind to pay."

I said, "The justice would charge me five dollars, but I will give you this," and I handed him a ten-dollar gold piece. Fourteen days after my wedding the quartermaster sent for me to start on a trip.

CHAPTER XI.

PLAINS LORE—HUNTING ADVENTURES.

COL. JOSEPH E. JOHNSTON had returned with orders to open a road from San Antonio to the head of the Llano. We made this trip, which was without any special incident. When we returned to San Antonio, Brigadier General Persifer Smith had arrived, and was in command of the department. One day he sent for me to come to his headquarters and asked me a great many questions about my knowledge of the country, and if I knew the heads of the different water courses. I told him that I had been only to the head of the San Saba.

"Can you tell the signs of water when you are out on the plains?"

"Yes, sir; I can."

"What are they?"

"Well, sir, there are a great many signs of water: the trees, the trails, the doves, the butterflies, and the wild animals."

"Well, that's pretty good; but how do you tell by these things?"

"Well, sir, wherever there are willow trees or pecan trees, there is most sure to be water. The trails of the wild animals, like deer and antelope, lead to water. The doves are never very far from water."

"How far?"

"Well, sir, four or five miles; maybe sometimes they might get six miles from water."

"How can you tell when a dove is going to the water or coming from it?"

"When a dove is going to the water, it flies above the tops of the bushes and trees and goes as straight as a bee to its hive; and when it gets to the water, it drops right down at the place. When it is going away, it flies zigzag, and stops carelessly along."

"Very well," he said; "and the butterflies?"

"Wherever there are large numbers of yellow or whitish butterflies and they rise in the air and dance up and down, as they sometimes do, they are near water, and they can be seen quite a long distance."

"If you found a trail of the wild animals, how could you tell which direction to take to go to the water?"

"You have to follow a trail only a little way to know which way the water is. If you are going from the water, the trail gets dimmer and dimmer, and other trails branch out from it until it fades out. If you are going to the water, the trail gets plainer and plainer all the time, and you will see other trails coming into it."

"Well, that will do, Polly. I want you to go with me. I am going to the head waters of all the rivers to the north of us as far as to the Trinity, and you are to be one of my guides."

"All right, General," I said.

The day before we were to start I was very sick. I went to the general and told him I was. I had a high fever.

"Go and see the surgeon, Polly, and see what he says."

The surgeon told me I was too sick to go, and gave me some medicine. I went and reported to the general, but I said: "General, I know I can go."

"You had better not go if the doctor says not, Polly."

"General, I know I can go, and as soon as I get into the woods I shall be better. I'll be bad sick if I stay here."

"If you get very sick, what will I do?"

"You can leave me."

"No, sir; I could not do that. But go and tell the doctor to give you some medicine, and you can take it as you go along."

The doctor was very angry when I told him what the general said, but he gave me the medicine, and said that I would get the whole party into trouble and myself too; that I was going to be sick.

About ten o'clock next morning we started. I was sick. When we got into the mountains, I got a lot of wild grapes and ate them. We camped on the San Jerónimo. There were about twenty-five of us. That night I had a high fever. I did not take the doctor's medicine. I got about half a teacupful of salt and put it in water and took it. There was a heavy storm coming, and we had no tents. I sat there in the rain on my saddle, O so sick, but that salt vomited me all night long. Next morning the general asked me how I was, and when I told him I was nearly well, he was very glad. I had no fever, and the second day the general called me to him and said: "Polly, I'm going to put you in charge of the packers and guides."

"General," I said, "I hope you won't do it. Here is Pedro Espinosa, an old guide, and a man who has been ten years a captive among the Indians, and knows all about them, and he's the best woodsman I ever saw."

"What I have ordered, Polly, I have ordered."

And I was put in charge of the packers and guides. Until we passed the head of the San Saba there was plenty of water. Beyond that we camped one night without water. We stopped about two hours by sun, and the general said to me: "Polly, take as many guides as you want, and see if you can find water."

"Pedro Espinosa is all I want," I said. I sent him out to the left, and I went to the right. I rode seven or eight miles without any sign of water. Then I saw I was not more than a mile and a half or two miles from water, and I turned back and made my report. I said: "General, I did not go to water, but I went within about two miles of it."

"Can you go there in the morning?" he asked.

"O yes, sir; I can go to it."

"Very well; we will go then."

Pedro Espinosa did not find anything.

Next morning we went to the water and camped all day by a beautiful little lake. In the evening I said to Lieutenant Dodge: "Lieutenant, let's go turkey-hunting."

"All right, Polly, we'll go."

We were going along a little trail, the lieutenant some distance in front, when I called to him: "Lieutenant, don't you see those turkeys running along there ahead of you?"

He saw them, a whole drove, running along single
file in the trail, a little downhill and at a pretty distance from him. The lieutenant was very tall. He
raised his shotgun and fired one barrel, and with that
single shot killed seven turkey gobblers. I never saw
such a shot. He struck them all in the head. I just
shouted at the sight. He took four and I took three.
They were very large, fat fellows, and we had a big
load back. I told the general that the lieutenant killed
them all at one shot.

"Well," said he, "I never heard of such shooting as
that; and you didn't kill any?"

"No, sir; the lieutenant loaded us down at one
shot."

On this trip we saw many parties of Indians. They
came to us at intervals, and, as we were few, they
thought there must be many more behind, and asked
me if there were not. At last, a lot of Indians came
up near us, and four or five came into our camp.
They asked the general to give them some beeves.
He asked how many they wanted, and they said three.
The general ordered the butcher to let them have
them. They began shooting at the ones selected, but
they couldn't shoot, and had the beef cattle all running wild. The butcher came to the general and said:
"General, I understand your guide is a good shot, and
I'd like for you to send him to shoot the beeves for
these Indians; they are stampeding all my cattle, and
can't hit anything."

I was lying in my tent. The general said: "Go
and ask him to do it. He's in his tent."

The man came and asked me if I would please go

and shoot the beeves for the Indians, as he understood I could shoot.

"All right," I said; "I'll go."

I took my gun and went with him. They had the cattle rounded up, and I said: "Which one do you want."

"That red one there."

I raised my gun and shot it down. I loaded and said: "Where's the next?"

He pointed it out, and at the crack of my gun it fell. I loaded again, and asked for the other. He showed it, and I downed it like a flash. You should have seen those Indians look at me. They came up around me and took hold of me, and felt of my arms and legs, and looked at my gun and talked about me to each other in their dialect. The chief offered me three horses for my gun.

I said: "No."

"I'll give you four," he said.

"No," I repeated.

"I'll give you five fine horses," he said.

"No; I won't sell my gun for five horses."

"I'll give you six big, fine horses."

"No, sir."

"I'll give you seven," he said.

"I'll not sell you my gun; you might kill me some day with my own gun."

On this same trip I saw General Smith looking up at the sky one evening, and he said: "What kind of weather do you think we are going to have, Polly?"

"General, there's going to be a great change in the weather."

"How do you know?"

"As I came along I heard a wolf howling over on the hill, and the wolf stated it. The wolf said that there would be a big change in the weather."

He burst out in a big laugh and said: "When is it to be?"

"I don't know that exactly, sir; but the wolf said it wouldn't be long—sometime to-night."

That night we had a terrible storm about midnight; a terrible wind. It blew the general's tent down. He called to me: "Polly, are you awake?"

"Yes, sir."

"Well, that was a wise old wolf of yours. Did your tent blow down?"

"No, sir; I tied it up strong and dug a ditch around it."

"Sergeant of the guard, send some men here to put up my tent." The men came running, and put up the general's tent.

General Smith left us shortly after this, and went in his carriage to visit some points farther north and east. He joined us at Fort Worth, and we shortly proceeded to San Antonio. After we reached San Antonio, the general sent for me to come to headquarters. When I got there, he said: "Polly, how long have you been in the service of the government?"

I told him.

"I want to keep you with me while I stay in this department, and I appoint you headquarters guide. You are only to go out when I go, or when I send you. Will you stay with me?"

"Yes, sir; I will stay with you; and I thank you very much, sir."

The general was always very kind to me. I never saw a man like him. He did more and with fewer men than any man I ever saw. He opened roads and established forts on the heads of all the rivers we went to. He was a great man. He decided to move head-quarters to Corpus Christi. San Antonio people were very mad about it, but he moved. I went with him, but I did not take my family. That was a mistake I made. Corpus Christi was almost the ruin of me. It was fandango after fandango every night, idleness and frolicking. The general told me that whenever I wanted to go hunting I could take an ambulance, a driver, and a cook. Game was plenty. What a time we had!

The general had to go to San Antonio in a great hurry on one occasion. He sent me on ahead with his carriage, and charged me to be ready for him at day-light next morning on the other side of the Nueces. We bogged down in a creek, and did not reach our camping place till one o'clock in the morning. We slept a little late, and were eating breakfast when the general came up to the river. He was in an army ambulance. I told the driver to take his carriage down to the ferry and be ready for him when he came over. The fellow left the mules unhitched and came back-for his breakfast. The noise of the ferry scared the mules, and they started, not running but walking. They went over a stump a yard high and broke loose from the carriage. The general saw it, and O he was the maddest man! He did not often swear,

5

but he swore then." "Where's Polly?" he said. "Tell him to come here."

I came up.

"What's the reason you were not ready here?"

I explained that we were up nearly all night, working to get out of the bog, and we were late getting through breakfast.

"That's nothing," he roared. "You ought to have been ready. Get away from here."

He ordered the driver to go on with the big ambulance.

"But, General, what shall I do with the carriage?" I said.

"Let it go to hell." And away he went.

The doubletree of the carriage was broken, and I had some new small rope. I pulled my big knife and cut two short, stout pieces of wood about eighteen inches long. I wrapped the two pieces very tight and close on both sides of the broken doubletree, and then I wet the ropes. It made it as strong and solid as if it were not broken. I jumped in and went at full tilt. The general's mules were strong and fast, and I overtook him before he got three miles away. His driver told him that I was coming with his carriage.

"What!" he said.

I drove up, and the general was smiling. He was over his passion, and I was glad.

"Well, have you fixed the carriage, Polly? Do you think it is strong enough to take me to San Antonio?"

"Yes, sir; it is," I said.

He got into the carriage and said: "I'm going to San Antonio, but you come on leisurely."

It was eighty miles to San Antonio, and he got there that evening. I expected to be discharged when I got there. He discharged his driver, but he did not discharge me. He had seen how quickly I fixed that carriage.

From Corpus Christi we were sent to the Rio Grande to take some things down the river in boats. I had my dog with me. He was one of the best dogs I ever saw. When we got to the river, one of the men said: "Whose dog is that?" (The man did not like me.)

I said: "He's mine."

"No dog can go in a boat with me," said the fellow.

"If my dog can't go, I can't," I said.

He swore he should not go in the boat. If the dog went, he would not. I went to the lieutenant in command and I said: "Lieutenant, that fellow says my dog shan't go in the boat. If my dog can't go, I can't."

The fellow was listening to us. The lieutenant said: "Put your dog in, Polly; and if he don't want to stay in the boat with him, he can get out."

The fellow always had a grudge at me after that, and one time when I was dancing he stepped up behind me and struck me such a blow that he knocked me senseless. My friends knocked him down, and we had a big row at that fandango.

CHAPTER XII.

GENERAL SMITH'S TRIP TO EL PASO.

General Smith went to El Paso in 1854, and took
an escort of forty men. Captain Walker was in command of the escort. I was headquarters guide. As
we came back we met a lot of men with cattle. They
were on their way to California. They said that the
Indians had stolen about forty of their cattle; that they
came and took them—rode up boldly and drove them
away right before their eyes, and they thought that if
the general would send some men, they could overtake
the Indians and get the cattle. The general said to the
captain that he could take all his escort and go after
the Indians. The captain came to me and said: "Polly,
tell the general you want to go with us."

"No," I said; "I won't tell him anything; if you
want me to go, you tell him you want to take me."

"Well, I'll tell him I want to take you, and that you
want to go."

"All right," I said; "tell him."

He went to the general, and I heard him say: "Polly
says he wants to go with us; can he go?"

"If he wants to go, he can."

We started right away. It had rained just before
the Indians took the cattle, and we could trail them
and go at a gallop. I waited for the captain to take
the lead, but he would not. He said: "I know nothing about trailing; you go ahead."

We went all day, and, as the moon shone, we went
on till it got cloudy and the moon went down. Then

we made camp and slept awhile, and, starting again as soon as we could see the trail, we soon saw a lone Indian on a mule. As soon as he saw us he jumped off and hid somewhere. It was mysterious how that Indian disappeared on the open plain. It was not long till we saw three or four Indians, and the captain sent Lieutenant Kerr and four or five men after them. Those Indians were after some of their own horses. When they saw us, they dismounted from the mules they were on and jumped on the loose horses, and without saddles or bridles escaped. We saw a bunch of Indian horses, and I went and rounded them up and drove them along with our pack mules and lead horses. I heard firing; too much for the four or five Indians and men, I thought, and told the captain so.

"Do you think so?"

"Yes, sir; I'm afraid the lieutenant and his men will all be killed; we had better send them relief."

"O there are only four or five Indians there."

I stood up on my horse and looked. I could see just over the low hill the camp of the Indians, and it looked like there were hundreds of them. I said: "Captain, if you will stand up, you can see. Our men will be surrounded and killed, and so will we if we stay here. Let's charge them."

"All right," said he; and away we went.

When we came up, the Indians ran. Lieutenant Kerr was wounded severely by an arrow. It struck him at the waist and glanced around under his belt, but did not go in very deep. He took hold of the arrow and pulled it out. He was sitting on the ground. The captain asked him if he was badly hurt.

"No, not mueh."

"Can you ride, lieutenant?"

"Yes, I can ride."

The Indians were running and yelling, going up the sides of the mountain. It looked like there were hundreds of them. Women and children were crying and yelling and climbing up the mountain side. They looked like so many old black buzzards swarming over the rocks. I noticed the Indian men were mounting their ponies and moving toward our right and left, and I sent word to the captain to come out to us, and I said: "Captain, these Indians are going to fight us."

"O, no; they're not."

"Yes, sir; they are. I know these Indians. They are going to fight for these horses of theirs we have caught, and we'd better get out of here. We can't fight them in here between these ridges. They have all the advantage. Let's get out of here, or we'll all be killed."

"Well, where'll we go?"

"Out there in that little open. We can form a circle around our horses and receive the Indians when they charge us."

We went to the place, dismounted, and formed a circle around our horses. The Indians were circling around us out of range. One of them called out in good English: "Come on if you want to fight."

One fellow on a fine horse kept riding out and coming a little nearer. He had a big pair of buffalo horns fixed on his head and a long bunch of feathers hanging down his back. I watched him awhile, and I said: "Captain, let me shoot that fellow."

"Can you hit him?"

"I think I can."

"Let him have it, then."

I leveled at him and fired. He yelled and leaned down over his saddle. A perfect uproar broke loose among the Indians. I never saw that fellow any more during the fight. I thought I shot him through the legs. They charged up · closer and rained arrows upon us. They shot their arrows angling upward and let them fall among us. They fairly rained all about us. One of our men was killed. Just as he raised his gun to shoot, an arrow struck him under the arm, passed through his body, and came out under the other arm. He was standing near me, and turned to me and said: "Polly, I'm shot."

He caught hold of the arrow and pulled it about half out and dropped dead. When the men saw that he was killed, they were almost panic-stricken. They started to run. I yelled at them: "Don't run; if you do, we'll all be killed. Come back! come back! we must stand together." I called to them till I was hoarse. I begged the captain to make his men fight. Some of them were so scared that they quit shooting. I talked ugly to the captain. I told him that he was not fit to be an officer. He was busy fighting himself; he was a brave man and so busy fighting he did not see the men about to run. I feared afterwards he would give a bad report of me to General Smith, but he didn't. In a few minutes the men came back. I was struck with an arrow just above the hip. I caught

hold-of it and pulled it out. A fellow crawled up behind some rocks and shot at me. The charge passed
so close to my ear it deafened me. . It must have been
an iron slug. I saw him, and I said, "O, I'll teach
you to shoot!" but my gun was empty, and he got
away!

After a time the Indians got their horses and drew
off and formed again farther off, and began calling
to us to come on and fight again. The men did not
want to go. They began saying: "Captain, we can't
go. without water; we are so thirsty and hot; let us
go and get some water." There was water about half
a mile away.

"What shall we do with this dead man?" asked the
captain.

Some said: "Leave him."

"No; we can take him with us," I said. "We
can lay him across this horse, and two can hold him
on while another leads the horse."

We did so, and went to the water. The Indians
came nearer and formed in ranks like soldiers, and
some one again called out in English for us to come
on and fight them. The captain asked who could fight
on horseback. I said I could. Three or four more
offered to fight on horseback, but again the men commenced saying that they were so tired they could not
fight; that the Indians were too many for them, and
showed so plainly that they did not want to fight
that the captain said: "Well, we'll give it up and let
them go." Then he said: "Men, get your swords here
and dig a grave, and let's bury this man."

I said: "O no, Captain; don't bury him here. It'll never do."

"Why not?" he asked.

"Why, Captain, the Indians will come up and dig him up and scalp him and hack him to pieces, and dance around him, and carry on like mad wolves over him."

"Well, what can we do with him, Polly, if we don't bury him?"

"Why, let's tie him on his horse and take him away from here, and bury him where they can't get him."

After I had made him see how we could do it, he consented, and we laid the poor fellow across his saddle and tied him on his horse and started. We traveled all that night and next day. The Indians did not follow us, and we buried our comrade where we did not think they would ever find him. We dug a grave with our swords, and buried him on an elevation, and leveled the grave over so that they would not see it, and left him there. I guided the company across the country by the course of the wind only. I had never been over that immediate country before, but I struck the passes and kept the right course until we overtook General Smith and the men with him. We went on back to headquarters at Corpus, and General Smith gave me a furlough for one month, and I went to spend it with my family in San Antonio. After I got back the general went to Aransas Harbor to receive a cargo of horses for his troops. When they were landed, he said to me: "Polly, I'm going to give you a horse. Go in among them and take your choice."

I went and looked at them all, and I took a fine bay. He was a beauty. The general asked me if I had taken a good one, and I said, "General, I believe he is the best horse in the lot," and I believe he was. I must tell about him. I trained him to hunt. That horse had more sense than many a man. I trained him to hunt deer, and when I said "Deer" I could dismount and send him toward the deer. The deer were used to wild horses and did not run from him. He would go slowly up toward them, feeding and stopping along, and I would crawl with my gun in hand behind him. When in range he would stop and look back at me, as much as to say: "Now shoot."

Once we saw some deer, and the general said: "Now, Polly, you are always bragging about that horse and how you hunt with him. Let's see you go after those deer yonder."

I started, the general and all the officers watching me with their glasses. When in a quarter of a mile of the deer, I dismounted and started my horse toward them, and I crawled behind. After some time my horse stopped and looked back at me. I raised up, fired, and killed one. The other jumped and ran a little way. I reloaded and fired again, killing that one too. I had killed both as fast as I could load. The general and the officers were astonished, and said that they had never seen anything like that.

Soon after this—in 1855, I think it was—General Smith was ordered East, and left the department of Texas. He offered to take me with him, but I told him that I did not want to leave Texas; that I had my family here; that I knew this country and did not

know that; that I could be very little use to him there,
and I could be useful in Texas. So I stayed. General Smith was a great man. He always treated me
with very great kindness. He took special pride in
my hunting and shooting. I learned many things
from him, and owe him much. He used to ask me
to his table to eat with him, much to the surprise of
the other officers. I can never forget General Persifer Smith.

CHAPTER XIII.

BEARS, INDIANS, AND A NIGHT RIDE.

AFTER General Smith left Texas, I remained again
in the employ of the quartermaster department with
Major Belga. It was decided to establish a camp on
the San Antonio River at a crossing in Wilson County,
where the Indians crossed whenever they came into
the country on their horse-stealing raids. It was
about fifty miles below San Antonio, and was called
Conquista Crossing. We were there in all about six
months. No Indians came that way while we were
there. By some mysterious means they knew of our
presence there, and avoided the place. I contracted
chills at Conquista Crossing, and was ordered to go
to Camp Verde with Captain Palmore, of the Second
Cavalry. Camp Verde was about sixty miles north-
west of San Antonio on a branch of the Guadalupe.
This was in 1856. While there a man (Dr. Nowlin),

came into camp and said that his horses had been stolen. A party was detached to go after the Indians. I went as guide. The doctor and his brother went along. We followed close after the Indians for several days.

We were out of fresh meat, and one day I saw a fat bear in the open plain, and I said: "Sergeant, let me go and kill that bear. We've got no fresh meat."

"All right," he said.

"Let me have your horse, won't you? Mine is jaded and run down by hunting this trail back and forth." .

He had a fine, fresh horse, and he let me have him. I started after the bear. I came up near him, but that horse flew back and started as hard as he could run, and I could not control him. He made a great circle round and I brought him again toward the bear, but he broke again and made another circuit with me. The sergeant had no rope on his saddle, or I would have tied the horse and followed the bear on foot; but I could do nothing with that fool horse, and the bear got into the brush and got away from me, and I had to go back without him. O, I was so mad at that horse!

We saw a party of Indians ahead of us one day, and thought they were the Indians we were after. I went ahead with another man, and the men followed on. When near enough I called to the sergeant to charge into them. They were cooking, and had not yet seen us. They broke and ran, leaving their arms and everything they had. For some reason our men did not come up, and one of the Indians—the chief, I suppose

—called the others back and they came slipping back and picked up their arms and aimed at me. I was calling to the man with me to keep moving about so they could not get aim at him and shoot him, and hallooing to the sergeant to pitch into them. He and his men commenced firing from their horses. The sergeant had never been in an Indian fight before. I said: "Sergeant, dismount the men and fight on foot, and I will go after the Indians' horses and pack mules."

I started after the horses and got them while the men were shooting at the Indians. When I got back I saw one of the soldiers, a man named MacDonell, a big man and a bully, always fussing and bullying among the men, standing behind a tree, and not fighting at all. I said: "Sergeant, look at MacDonell behind that tree. Make him come out from there and go to fighting."

The sergeant ordered him out, and abused him for being a coward; but that man never moved: he stayed right behind that tree, the coward! Our men moved around a little to get at the Indians, and left our horses exposed, and two Indians on foot started after them. I said: "Sergeant, those Indians will get our horses if we don't stop them."

The bugler, Jim Tafolla, saw the Indians after our horses, and started to meet them. I called to him that he would get killed, but he went galloping right after those two Indians, shooting at them with his pistol. The Indian in front had a shield on his arm, and I could see when the bullets hit the shield that they knocked up the dust close around him as they

glanced off. These shields are made of several thick-
nesses of rawhide, and get so tough and hard that
unless a bullet strikes them very square and solid it
will glance off. Tafolla kept advancing and shooting.
The Indian kept his shield whirling from side to side,
and the bullets glanced off. When close up, Tafolla's
pistol refused to fire; a cap had caught, and the cyl-
inder would not revolve. The Indian shot with his
bow and Tafolla struck at his head with his pistol.
The Indian dodged down and escaped. Tafolla had
an overcoat rolled up and tied on the front of his
saddle. The arrow struck it and cut about fifty holes
in it, and the arrowhead entered Tafolla's body just
inside of the hip bone. The Indian started back, but
kept turning his head and watching to see if Tafolla,
whom he evidently thought he had killed, would fall.
The other Indian must have been wounded; he went
back first, but did not hop so lively as when he came.
The main body of the Indians had got behind some
ledges of rocks right on the bank of the little lake, and
it was hard to get at them. The sergeant said to
me: "Polly, do you think we can get those Indians?
What do you think we'd better do?"

I said: "Sergeant, you'll lose two or three men
before you get them."

"Well, we'll let them alone; we've got their horses
and the things they left in camp. Come on, men; let
'em go."

Just before we drew off from them, Dr. Nowlin,
who had been shooting at the Indians, had his horse
shot down while standing very near it loading his
gun. He and the others then moved farther away.

The doctor was anxious to get his saddle, bridle, and rope off the dead horse. No one would volunteer to go with him. I said: "I will go, Doctor, but let some one come out here and take care of these horses."

We started. I said: "You understand the fastening of your saddle, so you take it off, and I will get the bridle and rope."

We stooped as low as we could, and made quick work of it, the Indians firing at us all the time, but none of them hit us. In this encounter we got five horses besides some pack mules, a number of buffalo robes, belts, moccasins, and other accouterments. One of our men, Martin, was pretty badly wounded by a gunshot. When I came up, the lower part of his lungs were hanging from the wound. He said: "Polly, do you think I am very badly wounded?"

I tried to encourage him, and said: "O no, Martin, I hope not; sit down here and we will do something for you.'"

The sergeant decided to go to Fort McCabet (still standing), in San Saba County, about forty miles away. I had never been there, nor had I ever been in the country just where we then were. The sergeant said that he would fasten a buffalo robe between two horses and let it swing and place Martin on it, to carry him to the fort. The robe was fixed and Martin was placed on it, but after two or three miles he said he could not stand it to travel that way; it shook and jolted him so the pain was very great. I said: "Sergeant, the best way to fix him will be to let him ride and put the lightest man we've got up behind him to hold him."

It was so arranged, and Tafolla, whose wound did not hurt him much and who was a very small man, got up behind, and we carried him that way to the fort. It was late in the evening when we started. I knew the direction, and took the lead. When night came on it was very dark and cloudy; we could see nothing, but the southeast breeze was blowing, and while it lasts it keeps the same course. So I guided myself after dark by the breeze. I kept my course so that the breeze was all the time on my right cheek. This took me in a northeast course. It was a long, dark ride, and the men kept asking me how far it was and bothering me with no end of questions, till I said: "Sergeant, you must make the men stop talking to me. I don't know this country. I am traveling by the wind. I can see nothing, and they are bothering me so that I shall soon know nothing."

The sergeant said: "Men, don't another man speak to Polly. You bother him so he'll never get us out of here. If another man speaks to him, I'll tie him to his horse's tail and make him walk to the fort. Let Polly alone."

Not another man spoke to me after that threat. About one o'clock the moon rose. A little later we saw some large, white object far ahead of us. The sergeant said: "What's that, Polly?"

"I don't know, but I think that's the fort."

An hour later we saw it was the fort, and were soon there. The men were so glad they hugged me and lifted me and carried me around. I had kept my course exactly, and come straight to the fort. But in spite of our relief, poor Martin died an hour after

we got there. The doctors at the fort held a post-
mortem, and found that he could not possibly have
lived even with the best of care. He was shot through
the top of the stomach, the alimentary canal being cut.

CHAPTER XIV.

Locating a Ranch.

From Fort McCabet we returned to Camp Verde,
where we remained a few days, when there came a
report that the Indians had stolen a few horses and
passed below Camp Verde, and we started after them.
The second day we were near them; I saw the camp
of the Indians. A sergeant was in command of our
squad. It was late in the evening. I proposed that
we leave our horses with two men, and slip up on them.
We were so near, I feared if they caught sight of us
they would escape before we could reach them. We
went along in the bed of a dry creek very stealthily,
till we were right under the high bank and they were
above us. We were so close under them we could
see their shields hanging on the limbs above us. We
went back a little to get up the bank. I was in the
lead, and in getting up I got my foot tangled in
some briers. The man just behind me stepped by
me and jumped right out in front of the Indians. He
was a splendid shot, but had never seen an Indian.
He leveled his gun at one who was cutting meat and
shot him dead, hitting him right in the lower end of
the nose. I got loose and ran out; the Indians were

6

all running and jumping over the bluff. I fired at one, and he left a bloody trail. I was sorry afterwards that I shot him. It was not necessary, as they were already all running. We got the things they left in their camp; but their horses were farther on in a thicket, and, as it was now nearly dark, we feared some one of us would get shot if we went into the thicket after the horses. We returned to our own horses, and next morning came again; but the Indians had also been back and carried off the dead Indian, and also got away with their horses. I told the sergeant that it would be useless to follow them, as they would scatter and we should be able to do nothing. I had scalped the dead Indian before we left him the evening before, because a lady at Camp Verde said to me as I was leaving: "Polly, bring me a scalp."

I took it to her, but she would not have it. She said in a very frightened voice: "I don't want it. I didn't think you would kill an Indian."

I had brought also a beautiful shield and a quiver full of arrows. The quiver was made of panther skin, with the animal's tail hanging from the lower end. The arrows and bow were beautifully carved and painted. I gave them to one of the officers who begged them of me.

I had hardly got back to camp when Captain Palmer said: "Polly, the camels have all got out and gone, and I want you to go after them."

"Well, Captain," I said, "let me rest awhile. I'm just back. Let me rest to-night."

"Well, you can rest to-night; but you must start early in the morning."

I started early with eight soldiers, and went by Bandera, struck the Medina River and went down it to the mouth of Privilege Creek, and there struck the trail of the camels and followed it up that creek. We were close on the camels when our dogs got after a bear. I went up on the ridge and presently I saw the bear coming directly toward me. I shot him dead. We went on and started another bear in a little time. I followed it and killed it also. We found two deer also right on the trail of the camels, and killed them. In a little while we came up with the camels and got them all. We were loaded down with bear, deer, and turkeys. We spent two days in camp on Privilege Creek. I liked the place so well that I said: "I'm going to find out who owns this land, and buy it and start a place here."

The men laughed at me and said: "O, you'll never leave the service of Uncle Sam."

"You'll see," I said.

When I got to camp, the captain was so glad to get the camels back that when I asked for a furlough he willingly gave it. I wanted to go to San Antonio and see about that land. There was so much game on it that I determined to get it if possible. As I entered the door of the surveyor's office I met Mr. James, a friend of mine, who asked me where I was going, and I told him I wanted to find who was the owner of the land on Privilege Creek. He said he was. I told him that I wanted to buy some of it, and he sold me three hundred and sixty acres for fifty cents an acre. This was in 1858.

To establish a place, I took my father out first from

San Antonio that I might, by his help, decide where
I should build my house. He was pleased with the
place, and we selected a site for the house, which I
at once built. I did not move my family there, but
kept them at Camp Verde, and put a Mexican family
in my house at the ranch. I could not get a title to
my land until after nine years of delay and trouble.
The State authorities refused to make a title, as it was
not surveyed according to regulations. But by dividing it up and changing the survey, Mr. James finally
got me the title. I afterwards moved my family to the
ranch, and got permission to stay there on condition
that I should immediately go to camp when sent for.
This arrangement continued until 1861, when the State
of Texas seceded from the Union. The United States
troops left Camp Verde and the State, and we passed
under Confederate authority. It was a sad day for me
when I had to part from the United States troops. I
had been with them for twelve years, and I had seen
much hard service with them, and had many good
friends among them. Major Wait was in command,
and asked me to go away with them, but I could not.
It would have been to leave everything behind, and
really forsake my family and home.

CHAPTER XV.

OUT OF THE ARMY—CIVIL WAR.

THE Confederate authorities at San Antonio secured for me a commission as captain in that service and sent for me and offered it to me. But I declined. My heart was really with the United States, that I had served so long.

They accused me of being a Union man. I said: "Now, it is like this: If I were out with ten men and nine should decide against me, I would be compelled to accept their decision. The State has seceded, and I accept the situation; but if I could have had my way, it would not have done so."

So I went back to my home and joined the "Home Guards." We elected one of my neighbors, a Mr. Mitchell, captain. It was our business to defend the neighborhood from the wild Indians and to keep down the disorderly element at home. I served four years, the whole period of the war, in this company. We were almost constantly on the scout, and had many unimportant encounters with the Indians. On one occasion, when camped on the head waters of the Llano, we found two men who had been starving for nine days. One of them came into camp. He was a fearful-looking object; barely able to walk, he was so feeble, and nothing but skin and bones, he was so nearly dead. We gathered around him, and he told us there were three of them together. They had deserted the Confederate service out West and were traveling together when they came unexpectedly into an Indian camp. The Indians fired on them and killed one of their number. The other two left everything and fled into the brush, and so escaped, and had been wandering for nine days with nothing to eat but two young crows which they found in a nest. These they ate raw. They had no means of making a fire. The man who came alone into camp told us his companion was about two miles back under a bluff. He had left him there, as he could walk no farther. A party of us went back to search for him, and found the place described to us, but could not find the man. We called out and explained that we were his friends; that we had his friend in our camp, and meant him no harm. At last he answered us, and came out from under the bluff where he had been hiding, fearing we were enemies seeking his life. We put him on a horse and carried him to camp, having given him a small piece of bread. The captain had to put a guard over them to keep them from killing themselves eating. They were as ravenous as wild animals. We did not let them have all they wanted for about three days. In that time they had begun to change wonderfully. They were sound and well soon, and Captain Mitchell gave them up to the Confederate authorities. He was a great friend of the Confederacy, and did all he could to help them.

Once during this service I asked the captain's permission to take my sister over into Mexico to her husband, who was over there. He gave it, and I took her and came back by way of San Antonio. I had bought a fine buckskin suit over in Mexico, and a fine Mexican hat, beautifully fixed up in Mexican style.

I was around a place of resort, a gambling and drinking place, one night, intending to leave early next morning for camp. The provost marshal for some reason (he was a bad man, a Captain De Hammond) attacked me. He demanded to know where I was from and where I had been. I told him a straight story—that I had permission from my captain to be absent—and he wanted to see my permit. I told him it was only verbal.

"That won't do," he said. "You'll have to go to jail."

I told him that was a place I never had been, and I was not going.

He said I would, and told the guard to take me. I determined to die rather than be put in jail. I offered to bring him any security from the best men in town. Nothing would do; I must go to jail. I was fully determined to kill him and die myself before I would go to jail. While the altercation was going on, an old man, Antonio Manchaca, who had known me from a child, and who was a kinsman of De Hammond, came up and took my part. He told De Hammond who I was, and that whatever I said was right. So the provost marshal let me go. Next day I started home, and as I went along I made up my mind never to go into another gambling hole as long as I lived. I gambled after that, but I never again went into a gambling resort.

When the war ended our company of home guards was disbanded, and in a few months the United States troops returned. They had heard of me, and the company that was camped on Bandera Creek near the town sent for me and offered me a hundred dollars a month to join them and act as guide and escort. I could not accept the offer, as I had so enlarged my place and had so many interests on my hands—stock of all kinds—and was making money trading. I recommended my cousin, James Tafolla, and he went, but he did not remain long in the service. I then recommended an American, William Valentine, who stayed with them some time. He was a good woodsman, and knew how to trail. It takes a keen, smart man to trail; not many can do it. Experience is necessary. A trailer must not look along under his feet, but keep the trail far ahead of him, by signs he must notice, by broken twigs and weeds. A good trailer can ride at a gallop. I have trailed where every other man said there was no sign, and would not believe I was on the trail until we came upon the Indians. The Indian is very smart to cover up his trail. I don't know anybody that can equal him.

I remained on my ranch attending to my business for the next ten years or more, making money all the time. During this time I gave close attention to agriculture, and took the premium two years in succession at the San Antonio fair for the best display of farm products.

CHAPTER XVI.

THE PROTESTANTS—CONVERSION.

JAMES TAFOLLA, my cousin, now lived in the same neighborhood with me on Privilege Creek. He had been educated in Georgia, and had been a bugler in the army, and when he settled down after the war he was elected a petty officer of the peace, and although, like the rest of us, he had been pretty wild, he wanted to do better as an officer. He was already at heart a Protestant, though he had never declared it to us, as we were all Catholics. Such a thing as a Protestant Mexican was unknown then. Some of our Mexicans were Masons (I was one myself), but not Protestants. Tafolla organized a society, which was for mutual help and instruction. It met once a month on Sunday in the neighborhood schoolhouse. It had a regular constitution and by-laws. Tafolla was president and I was secretary. We kept regular minutes, and opened our exercises with prayer. I recollect that I translated into Spanish out of the Masonic books a form or two of prayer for the use of the society. We read from the Bible, and also stood up and read the prayers from the book. We had debates and discussions. The attendance was good. Most of the men of the neighborhood belonged to it. I said one time to Tafolla: "Something great is going to come out of this society; no telling where it is going to."

This society went on till a Mexican Protestant preacher, named José Maria Casanova, came into the neighborhood preaching. He preached at the schoolhouse. I was opposed to his preaching there. I did not go to hear him, and tried to stop it. We accused Tafolla of bringing the preacher there, and the disagreement among us broke up the society. Soon after this Tafolla joined the Methodist Church. The first time he came to my house after that I asked him if he had joined the Protestants, and he said that he had.

"Well," I said, "you can't come into my house any more; I want you to keep out."

"Do you mean it?" he asked.

"Yes, I mean it."

"Well, very well. Good evening," he said, and left.

Sometime afterwards I was out in the woods and met him. I was going to pass him without speaking, but he spoke first, and I just barely spoke and passed on. After he went by a few steps he called to me and said that he was going away and would sell me a filly he had. That interested me, for I was always ready for a trade. He named the price, and I told him I would give it, and the next day I went after the horse. There was a preacher there, Trinidad Armendariz. When I got near the house, they saw me coming; and as the preacher was about leaving and was going to have prayers before he started, they waited and asked me to join. I told Tafolla I was in a hurry. But he begged me to come in, and said that the preacher was going to pray before he started.

I said: "I didn't come here to pray; I came to get that filly."

But I went in. I was mad. I sat down with my hat on. I sat up while the preacher prayed, getting madder all the time. He prayed for me; he asked the Lord to touch my heart, to convert me, telling him that I was prominent in the neighborhood, and make me an instrument in the salvation of others.

When the prayer was ended, I went out of the house, and as soon as I could get the filly I left. I went home, but I could not forget that prayer. I passed a sleepless night. I got up in the morning feeling so wretched and miserable that I did not know what to do with myself. I could not throw it off. I saddled my horse and started to Bandera for the purpose of getting on a spree to drown my misery, for I never before had felt anything like it. I was anxious to throw it all off. But as soon as I entered the barroom the smell of the liquor was horrible to me. I stopped, and did not know whether to go in or not, but I went in and sat down on a bench. I was feeling awful. The fellows were calling me to come and join their games; but I said "No," and sat still. They asked me what was the matter.

"Nothing," I said; "only I don't play."

Several of them asked me to take a drink, but I said: "No, nothing for me."

At last Charlie Montague came in with a big crowd and said: "Polly, come on and let's take a drink."'

"No," I said; "I don't want it."

"What's the matter?"

"Nothing."

"Come and take a lemonade then," he said.

"Not even a lemonade," I answered.

"Why, Polly, what's the matter with you?"

"Nothing," I said.

Presently Charlie came to me and said: "Come, Polly, let's go home to dinner."

"No, I don't want any dinner."

"O, come on; we are going to have a fine dinner; it is Rosa's birthday."

"No, I don't want any dinner."

With that he slipped his arm through mine and lifted me up and said: "You *must* go."

"Well, I will go and feed my horse, but I don't want to eat myself."

We went to dinner and I couldn't eat. Charlie's father asked me if I was sick.

I said: "No; I am not sick."

"Well, what is the matter with you?"

"Nothing;" and I kept saying that and they kept begging me to tell what the matter was, especially the old man Montague, until at last I said: "I don't know what's the matter with me; but if you must know, I can tell you what has happened to me."

I then told them about going to buy the filly, and the preacher's praying the Lord to touch my heart, and I said it looked like he had done it; something had touched me; I never felt so bad in my life. The old man broke out on me, for he was a bitter Catholic, and said that if I was turning Protestant I should never come inside of his house again; if I turned my jacket and joined the Protestants, I should never sit down at his table. I told him that I did not say I was turning Protestant, but I had only told him what had happened to me and how I felt. He was very angry and bitter in his talk to me, so much so that Charlie finally said: "O pa, don't talk to Polly that way."

That made him more furious, and father and son soon got into a quarrel, and both got up from the table, and it looked like they were going to fight. While they were quarreling I went out and got on my horse and started home. I was as miserable as before, and the farther I went the worse I got. After I got close to Polly's Peak, a fine hill on Privilege Creek, going through the woods—for I didn't take any road —I felt so wretched that I got down off my horse and went off into the bushes and fell down on my face and prayed to God. I told him how miserable I was, and that if he would forgive me and save me I would be his humble servant the remainder of my days. I then got on my horse and started home. I soon commenced to feel better, and then better. I felt so light and free that I began to ride faster and faster. I was about a mile from home, and I made my horse go faster and faster—first a trot, then a gallop. I wanted to whoop. By the time I got home my horse was racing as hard as he could go. O, I can never forget that time! I had never felt that way before. I went into the house and kissed my wife and children. As I did not do that way usually, my wife looked at me very anxiously. She thought I was crazy. I went upstairs, and she followed me into her room. The walls were lined with images of saints and virgins, and I said: "My wife, take these things away."

"Why, what do you mean?" she asked me,

."The Lord has taught me that we must not bow down and worship these things."

She burst into tears and told the children that their father had gone crazy.

"No," I said, "I am not crazy; but I know we must not pray to these things."

That night I read from the Bible and prayed with my family, and from that day to this my house has been a place of prayer.

My conversion made a great sensation among my neighbors and friends; and as I was so completely changed, the report that I had gone crazy was believed by many. It was so different from anything they had ever heard of, and from any of their ideas about religion, that they could not explain it in any way except by saying that I had lost my reason. I was changed indeed. Nothing but the power of God could have done it. I talked to everybody about the need of the same great change that I had experienced.

CHAPTER XVII.

PERSECUTIONS.

My activity for Christ awakened opposition. I talked to everybody I came in contact with—Americans, Mexicans, and negroes. My own family were against me in it all. The great change in my life and the lessened attention I was giving to my ranch business caused the report that I was crazy to be be-

lieved by many people, especially among the Mexicans, who knew nothing about a change of heart and
life as a result of faith in Christ. But I went forward
with strength of purpose, calling on the Lord. I
wrote to my cousin, Tafolla, who was now preaching
at Laredo, whom I had driven from my house, telling
him of my conversion and asking his pardon for what
I had done, not knowing the fault I was committing.
He wrote me a beautiful letter in reply, glorifying God
in my conversion.

I talked often to one of my old friends, Arthur
Pugh, who used to drink and gamble with me. I
loved him, for he was a good man, honorable and
kind-hearted, though he had the vices common to us
all. He promised me he would quit it all, and did
for three months. Then he went back to the barroom in Bandera, and there came a stranger there—
a gambler—and Arthur gambled with him all day.
Late in the evening he at last won all that Arthur had,
and as he raked the money in some one made a sign
to Arthur that the man had some cards up his sleeve.
Arthur drew his pistol and leveled it at him and
cursed him for a cheating scoundrel, and told him to
shake those cards out of his sleeve. He shook his
sleeve and three aces fell out, and Arthur took back his
money. The man stood around awhile and went out.
After dark Arthur stepped outside the door, and while
standing there the man shot him in the dark without
warning. The ball struck him in the side. Arthur
turned toward the flash of the pistol, drawing his own
as he turned. As he turned around, the man fired
again. The ball struck Arthur in the breast below

the heart, and he fired at the same time. The bullet from Arthur's pistol struck the man in the eye and killed him on the spot. Arthur died next morning. If he had only kept his promise and stayed away from that saloon, my friend might have been alive yet.

My wife was honest in the opinion that I was crazy, and was besides very angry with me. For a whole year she never sat down at the table with me. I prayed continually for her and prayed in her presence, and it looked for a time as if she never would be converted. Brother Sutherland, who came to see me after my conversion, thought she was so bitter that she would never believe. But I carried my burden to the Lord, and was rewarded at last by seeing her converted. Yet she held out a long time. She said to the children one day in my presence: "Don't come here while your father is in this fix. The crazy old fool will get you to believing these ideas of his."

I prayed for her and talked very gently to her. I said: "Wife, if you don't want to live with me, we can separate. You can live on one ranch, and I will live on the other."

"No," she said; "I don't intend to do that."

"Well, then, let us not quarrel."

One day I heard her say to some women who were there: "He is another man!"

She commenced to read the Bible, and one day about a year after my conversion she said to me that she saw it was the truth. I told her to pray to the Lord for help. I had preached in my house one day when she said publicly she believed the gospel and made a beautiful prayer. I was very happy to see this change.

It was complete. She began to talk to everybody in favor of the gospel, and was an earnest believer. She said: "I want all the children to join the Church first, and then I will join. I want to be the last. You were the first; let me be the last." And so she did; after they had all become members, she joined too.

My neighbors and kin, among them my brother, José, used to come every night and gather on the bank of the creek across in front of my house and abuse and insult me in the most outrageous manner. They kept this up for a long time, trying to provoke me to some deed or word against them, but the Lord helped me to stand it all. They would curse and insult me and the Protestants and the preachers. All I did was to ask the Lord to help me and to stop them, and he did it. One of my brothers, Manuel, told the people that he was going to my house and beat me well for turning Protestant. He got to my house and tied up his horse just as I was ready to preach in the house to a few people. I said: "Sit down, brother; I am going to preach a short sermon, and then we will go and attend to your horse."

While I preached he listened. I saw that he was touched by the Spirit. The tears ran down his cheeks. At the end I said that if there were any there that believed the gospel for them to come and give me their hand. My brother got up trembling and gave me his hand. He had believed the gospel. Poor fellow, he was afterwards killed by his horse.

7

CHAPTER XVIII.

A PREACHER.

SEVERAL months after my conversion I went one day to Bandera and saw a crowd of people at the house of Pat Sena, and I asked what was going on there. Some one said that it was a Methodist Quarterly Conference. I went into the house and sat down. I should say that there was no Protestant church in Bandera, and their meetings were held in a private house. As I sat there looking on, some one asked me if I wanted anything. I said: "Yes; I want license to preach."

I was not even a member of the Church then. They looked at me with great astonishment. The presiding elder, Rev. J. C. Walker, said: "Why, aren't you a man who spends his time around the barrooms drinking and gambling? What do you want with a license to preach?"

I said: "I used to do that, but I have quit now."

After a little more talk he said to me: "Go out yonder and stay under those trees till we call you in."

I went out and they talked about me. Presently I was called in, and the presiding elder asked me why I wanted to preach. I then told the story of my conversion; and when I finished, the presiding elder turned to Brother Jimmie Hedgepeth, who was Secretary of the Conference, and said: "Brother Jimmie, write him a license to preach, and I will sign it."

He wrote it and handed it to Brother Walker, who signed it and handed it to me. It was dated April 14, 1877. Unfortunately, I afterwards lost it.

I went afterwards with Brothers Walker and A. J. Potter on several trips and preached to the Mexicans, and before much time had passed I had a visit from Rev. A. H. Sutherland, the superintendent of the missions of the Methodist Episcopal Church, South, among the Mexicans. He asked me if I had been baptized, and I told him I had not; and on his saying that I ought to be I said that I did not wish to be baptized, as I was satisfied with my baptism. He said that unless I was baptized he could not call me brother.

"Very well," I said; "I am satisfied with my baptism."

That night I occupied a room adjoining that of Brother Sutherland, and before retiring I read the third chapter of John. I did it not by design, and shall I say I did it by accident? The chapter convinced me that I should be baptized, and I thought of going and asking Brother Sutherland to get up and baptize me, but I thought I would wait until morning and not disturb him. So, as soon as he was up, I went to his room to tell him; but he was at prayer, and I retired. When he was through, he came into my room and asked if I wanted anything, and I said: "Yes; I want to be baptized." I told him what I had read the night before. So he baptized me that morning after morning prayers in my own home.

During that year I made two trips with him to Eagle Pass and labored among the Mexicans. We there met with Manuel and Andres San Miguel, who were afterwards converted, and who are now preachers in our Conference. I went to the Annual Conference at Corpus Christi, but could not be admitted, as I was not properly recommended by the Quarterly Conference.

I went back home and spent the year in preaching through the country round about my home, and made several trips with Brother Sutherland out West. I went to Eagle Pass and Guerrero, Coahuila, and neighboring towns, and preached the gospel to them.

CHAPTER XIX.

JOINS THE ANNUAL CONFERENCE.

IN the fall of 1878, being duly recommended, I went to San Marcos, Tex., and was admitted on trial into the West Texas Conference of the Methodist Episcopal Church, South. There joined with me at that time Alejandro de Leon, Roman Palomares, and Matilde Treviņo. I was sent to Bandera Mission, which included my home. During that year a number of people were converted and joined the Church, among them my son Luis and his wife. I commenced to plan the building of a church at Polly, my home. The next Conference met at Luling; and having preached one year as a local preacher and one as traveling preacher, I was ordained deacon by Bishop George F. Pierce, who held the Conference. At this Conference I was returned to Bandera, as I was for the three succeeding years. During this time I built the stone church that is still known in the neighborhood as Polly's Church. I cut the stone and hauled it myself during spare time from my duties as preacher in charge. I collected considerable sums of money among friends of mine, among them the Mavericks, of San Antonio. I found them all together one day, and four of these friends gave me twenty-five dollars each, and a fifth ten dollars. There were present George, Albert, Samuel, and William Maverick, and Mr. Terrell. Two of them offered to help me more if I should need it. James Hill, my son-in-law, furnished the lime for the church; my son Luis hauled the sand. At the dedication of the church, as at the laying of the corner stone, we had special services presided over by Rev. A. H. Sutherland, presiding elder of the district.

The dedication was of great interest to the whole neighborhood; we had a meeting of several days' duration. We brought our dinners to the place, and held three services each day. We received some new members, and the impression made on the community was deep and lasting. People came as far as twenty miles to be present at these services.

At the Conference held at Seguin, at the end of my third year as a traveling preacher, I was ordained elder by Bishop Linus Parker, who held that Conference. From the next Conference I was sent to Del Rio, Tex., having finished four years on the Bandera Mission. I had good success at Del Rio, and added many members to the Church. During the time I made a visit to Uvalde, and heard that an old friend of mine was very sick, and I went to see him. I found him very low. I asked him if he knew me.

"Yes," said he.

"Do you know my business?"

"Yes."

"Would you like for me to pray with you?"

"Yes; I would be glad."

I commenced to sing, and while doing so my friend's wife sent a boy from the kitchen to say that she did not want any praying in the house by me. I said to my friend: "Your wife doesn't want me to pray here."

"Pay no attention to her," he said. "Call the others here and let them kneel down."

And so we did, and, all kneeling around his bed, I prayed. When I had finished, he said: "I am glad you came."

I asked him: "Do you believe on our Lord Jesus?"

"Yes, I do."

"Trust in him, and you will be all right; that is all you have to do."

"I know I am all right," he said with joy.

"Give me your hand," I said, and he gave me his hand. I told him just to trust the Lord, and then said: "I must go; good-by."

I left him and was gone only a few minutes when a man passed me and said: "That sick man is dead."

How glad I was that I had gone to see him!

Once when I was in San Antonio there happened a very remarkable thing. I was in the blacksmith shop of Simon Peña when a man came running in greatly excited and said: "A man has been stabbed in the heart out yonder and is dying. Get this minister to go there to him." And he said to me: "Won't you go?"

"Yes, I will."

I went and found a crowd of people around him, and the women crying and bringing the images of saints and holding them to him. I said to them, "Take these things away from here," and in alarm and anger they moved away. I said to the man, who was badly cut: "I am going to read some verses out of this New Testament and pray for you; shall I?"

"Yes," he said; "do it."

I read and said to him, "Now I am going to pray just as if it were you praying for yourself;" and I confessed his sin and pleaded for his pardon for Christ's sake. When I finished, I said to him: "Do you believe on our Lord Jesus Christ?"

"Yes."

"Do you repent of your sins?"

"Yes."

"Do you trust in Christ to save you?"

"Yes."

I took his hand and he grasped mine with a strong pressure, and in that moment his head rolled to one side and he was dead, having made a good confession in his dying moment. I trust that he was saved.

CHAPTER XX.

IN LABORS ABUNDANT.

As I have said, the first four years of my active ministry were passed on the Bandera Circuit, within which my home on Privilege Creek is located. The remaining twenty, up to the time these incidents were recorded, were passed partly in Texas and partly in Mexico, as pastor at Del Rio, Guerrero, San Marcos, San Antonio, Luling, Zaragoza, Tobey, and Bandera. I shall not give a detailed account of all this time, but rather shall select at random a few interesting incidents.

Once while I was pastor at San Antonio, Tex., I had an encounter with Padre Antonio, a well-known priest there. I had known him for many years, from before the time of my conversion. A brother of mine had been killed by the kick of a horse, and I went afterwards to settle the bill for funeral expenses. When I reached the house of the friend, who in my absence had paid the bill for me, I found Padre Antonio there. He seemed afraid of me. I took his hand at the door, and he wanted to know if I was Mr. Rodriguez, from the mountain. I said I was, and he tried to pull away from me. I held his hand, and the women of the house showed alarm. I said to them all: "If you will allow me, I would like for us to have a few words on the subject of religion."

"Certainly, Mr. Rodriguez; anything you like."

I went in and we sat down. Padre Antonio talked in

a very rambling way and said nothing. When I attempted to speak, he would raise his hand and say: "Hold on; I'm not done yet."

At last I said: "Allow me to say a few words."

"Well, very few," said he.

I stood up and lifted up my right hand and said: "I believe in God the Father; I believe in Jesus Christ, our Saviour, and I believe in the Holy Ghost. I believe what Christ says: That nobody cometh unto the Father but by him. I believe he forgives sin; no one else can."

I went on quoting the Scripture, and he jumped up and fairly shot out of the door and went away. Adolfo Cardenas, then a new convert, was in my hack outside, and he rushed past without even looking at him.

Once after this I was traveling in my hack, and stopped for dinner. I had spread out my lunch when Padre Antonio drove up. I invited him to come and eat with me, and he said: "Thank you, I will."

He hitched his horse and came and sat down with me. I said, "I will ask a blessing," and did so.

He said: "That is very nice."

We talked along very pleasantly for a time about indifferent matters, when he said: "I want to ask you, Mr. Rodriguez, if your conscience does not hurt you for the way you do. You are leading many people astray and causing them to be lost."

I said: "*You* are the man that is leading them astray. You say you can save them, that you are able to forgive them; I tell nobody that. I tell them that only Christ can save them, and I point them to

Christ. I tell them to believe only in him; I lead nobody astray."

He got very angry and stopped eating.

"O," I said, "don't get mad; that is no use."

But he went to his buggy very angry. Presently he came back, and I asked him to continue his dinner.

He said: "No; I'm done."

He was in a great rage. He went back and forth from me to his buggy three times. I did not know what he was after. I went on quietly eating my dinner. He always avoided me after that.

I once made a preaching trip from Bandera to the Concho Creek. I was going to the house of an acquaintance to spend the night, when a boy, a distant relative of mine, saw me and came out to me and said: "Come, go home with me."

"No," I said; "I'm going to stay with Felix Flores."

"O, you needn't go there; the priest is there and a whole crowd of people; there's no room for you there."

"Well, I'll go; and if there's no room, I'll go back with you."

So I went on to Flores's house. When he saw me, he came out to me. I was sitting in my hack. He asked me to get out and stay with him.

"Have you got any room for me?" I asked.

"Yes, yes, there's room for you; get down and come in."

His wife came out also to speak to me and to ask me in. So I got out. All the people came up to speak to me, but the priest sat still. I walked up to him and shook hands with him. They asked me to supper, but I said I had just eaten and did not want supper. After they had eaten supper and were sitting around the table, I went into the dining room with my large Bible under my arm and said: "Felix, I always have prayers where I am after supper. Will you allow me to have prayers with you?"

"Certainly you can, Mr. Rodriguez; certainly."

The priest jumped up and said excitedly: "I'll have prayers."

"All right," I said; and he bowed down to pray. He prayed to the saints, the Virgin Mary, the angels, and never once mentioned our Heavenly Father nor our Saviour. After he was through, I said: "Now we joined you in prayer, won't you join me?"

"You're not going to pray in this house."

"I'll do so if the owner of it allows me. Will you let me pray here, Felix?"

"Yes; you can," said Felix.

"If you let that man pray in here, I'll leave; I won't stay here," said the priest.

"I let you pray here, and I'll let him pray too," said Felix.

"Well, I'll leave," said the priest, and he started out of the door.

Felix said to me, "Hold on a minute," and he followed the priest out. He told him he could not go away; the night was dark; his horses had been turned out to graze, and it was impossible for him to get away.

"I won't stay where that man is; I will leave."

"All right," said Felix; and he came back into the house and said to me: "Go ahead."

I read the Scriptures and prayed. While I was

praying I heard the step of the priest on the doorway coming back. He waited just outside till I had finished, when he pushed in and said: "You don't believe in God nor the mother of God, nor in the saints."

"I believe in the Father and the Son and the Holy Ghost, and no more," I said.

"You don't believe in the mother of God?"

"God has no mother," I said, "and I can prove it to you by the Holy Scripture;" and I read the account of the annunciation by Gabriel to Mary, and the other scriptures about the Virgin, and showed him that she was only a holy woman elected to be the mother of Christ's human body. He said my Bible was false, and showed great anger, but also that he did not know the Scriptures. We talked and argued until three o'clock in the morning. The priest was greatly worried. He went often out to his buggy in the yard, and came back smelling strongly of whisky. We continued arguing. I showed him how to use the references of the Bible, and we searched out the Scriptures. He did not know where to look for the different books of the Bible, and could not understand how I could find my proofs so quickly. When we concluded at 3 A.M. he was nearly drunk, and the people were saying: "The priest has lost."

The next morning he wanted to buy my Bible, and I told him I would give him a small Bible, but that I had only one large one.

"No," he said, "I want the big one. I'll give you a dollar for it."

"It is worth two dollars."

"I haven't got the money."

"Well," I said, "I can't sell it for a dollar; but I'll give you the small, fifty-cent Bible."

He ran his hand into his pocket and handed me the two dollars, after saying he hadn't that much!

CHAPTER XXI.

CONTROVERSIES.

WHILE I was once on the Zaragoza Mission in Mexico, my presiding elder, C. A. Rodriguez, and I had an encounter with another priest. It was our quarterly meeting at Peyotes, a fanatical place where they adore an image of Christ called "El Niño de Peyotes." At the night service the presiding elder was preaching, when there was a great noise and loud talking outside. I went out to see what it was about. There was a man in his shirt sleeves, who was talking loudly, and I said: "My friend, do me the favor not to disturb us."

"I'm in the street, and I can do what I please," he replied.

"No, you cannot do what you please even in the street."

He bragged that he could do as he pleased.

"No, sir; you can't. We can have you arrested and take you to the justice for disturbing us."

He went away, and I went into the house. It was a rented house where we had our services. Presently the same man came in and sat down with his hat on. Brother Rodriguez asked him to please take his hat off.

He replied: "I paid $14.50 for this hat, and I'll wear it here or where I please."

Brother Rodriguez had the reform laws in his pocket, and pulled out the pamphlet and read the law about disturbing public worship, and said: "We can have you arrested for this disturbance."

He got up and went out, and called out as he did so: "All that are on my side, come out of here."

It was the priest of Peyotes. About half of the congregation followed him out. Some of our people went out with them to stop the mob. Brother Rodriguez went on preaching. They came near getting into a fight among themselves. They came to the house where we stayed and smeared the door with dung. That night they stole a tap off my hack; and when I started, the wheel of my hack came off. Brother Rodriguez said: "I'm going to prosecute this priest."

I said: "No, don't do that; just go to the justice and tell him what has happened." And he did so.

After we had gone, the priest made up a party to follow us. When he got on his horse to start, the horse ran away with him; the branch of a tree struck the priest on the breast, knocked him off and nearly killed him. He was drunk at the time. He was laid up many days. That ended the affair. He never bothered us any more. Before he was well he was sent away. He was a gambler and a drunkard.

While on this Zaragoza Mission Brother Sutherland came to visit us and brought his wife and three children. We all went back in my hack, and were traveling one night by moonlight. Suddenly Mrs. Sutherland pulled her husband's coat and pointed behind the wagon. There were two armed men who had come up, and their horses' noses were almost in the hind end of the hack. The men were looking in. When we observed them, they asked us where we were going. We said to Eagle Pass. Presently they dropped behind, and after a little they came galloping up with their guns in their hands. I was watching them. They were excited, and I could hear them breathing harder than their horses. I had my shot-gun in the hack. I reached down quickly and got it. Brother Sutherland was driving. I raised my gun in readiness. When they saw the movement, they leaned down on the necks of their horses and rushed by us. We held a brief consultation and decided to drive out in the bushes and pass the night. We did so. Brother Sutherland and I took turns at going on guard till daylight. We then proceeded, but saw no more of the men, who were evidently intent on robbing us—perhaps first killing us.

While on this mission I had four valuable horses stolen from me. I recovered two of them only in San Antonio, where they had been sold for eighty dollars.

There is another story of an encounter I had with a priest soon after my conversion which is worthy of a place here.

Padre Felix, a Pole, was the parish priest of my neighborhood. He had frequently said that he wanted to see me and talk with me. I heard he was to say

mass at a home three miles from my house, and I
went to the owner and asked him to ask Padre Felix
if he would talk to me publicly after he finished mass.

"O, I know he will," he said; "it is not necessary
to send him word."

"But," I said, "I want him to agree to it before-
hand, and then, if anything should happen, he could
not say I had come to insult him."

"All right, I'll send."

"And I'll come to-morrow to see what he says."

He consented to talk with me after the mass, which
was appointed for eight o'clock. I went before the
time. I was quite early, but he was nearly done when
I got there. I went in and kneeled down, not to the
mass, but to God. I said: "Father, I have always
needed thee, but never so much as now. Help me;
put words in my mouth for this time." I wept and
begged the Lord to help me. When the priest had
finished, I went up to him and said: "Well, father,
I'm ready."

"O, Mr. Rodriguez, you must excuse me. The man
with me here has been summoned on the grand jury,
and is in a great hurry, and I can't stay to talk with
you now."

"Very well," I said, "I'll excuse you; but I want
you to answer me three questions before you go."

"Very well; what are they?"

It was strange that I had not up to that moment
thought of asking him questions, and I had no questions prepared. I think the Lord gave them to me.
When he consented to hear me, I said: "Well, the first
one is this: Where does this word 'mass' come from?"

"From the Pope," he said.

"Then it is not in the Bible; it does not come from God?"

"No; what is the next question?"

"Where does the doctrine of celibacy come from? Is it from God's Word?"

"It is from the Pope."

"Then it is not from God, who made man and said that it was not good for him to be alone, and made a partner for him, taking a rib from the man's side to do it."

"What is your other question?"

"The other is not a question, but I want to tell you there is no such a thing as a priest now in the Christian Church."

"You can't prove that," he said with anger.

"I can;" and I read from my Bible as rapidly as I could the chapters in Hebrews about the priesthood of Christ. He listened, and the people crowded around and listened. When I finished, he broke out saying: "That Bible is false."

"No, it is not false; the Catholic Bible says the same thing. Have you a Bible?"

"Yes, but it is in Latin. Can you read Latin?"

"No, I can barely read my own language; but there is a Catholic Bible in Spanish, isn't there?"

"Yes, but I've not got one."

He affirmed three times in a loud and angry voice that my Bible was false. The people were much interested, and there was some excitement. I held my Bible up high in my hand and said to the priest: "My friend, I call on you here in the presence of

8

God and all these people to say if this holy Book of
God is a false book. If it is untrue, I want you to say
it so these people can hear."

"No, it is not false; but you have no right to have it."

"No right to have it! Does not our Saviour say,
'Search the Scriptures?' Doesn't he say it to everybody? He does not say, 'Felix or Polly or Peter,
search the Scriptures.' Then who has a right to this
book if I haven't? Why I have, and all the priest-
ood of God—that is, the people."

Upon this came the man of the house and said,
"Father, breakfast is ready," and started away with
the priest, who was now very mad. He was trembling
with excitement, he was in such a rage. He went
with Lopez, who had him by the arm; and when he
reached the doorway, he jerked loose from him and
whirled around with his hand extended as if to strike
and started toward me. The crowd was watching him.
I am sure his intention was to return and strike me.
There were some men standing in the doorway who
lived on my ranch; and when they saw him start toward me, they turned their quirts around in their
hands ready to use the heavy ends. I think they shook
them at him. He stopped short, looking at them,
with his open hand extended as if to strike. It is
well he didn't, for those were rough fellows, and he
would have felt the weight of the heavy ends of those
quirts. The women began to cry and scream in alarm,
and Lopez again took his guest by the arm and led
him off to breakfast, trembling with rage.

There belongs to this period another singular experience I had, but of a very different kind. I was

making a trip to the head of Mason's Creek, and at noon one day, as I was near a camping place, I came up with a man who had gone into camp and was about preparing his dinner. As I drove up and spoke to him I said: "There is a nice spring just ahead a little way, and there's no water here; why not hitch up your horses and drive on to the water? I'm going there, and we can camp together." He did so. When we reached the spring and had unhitched, he said to me: "What is your business?"

"I'm a preacher of the gospel."

"You are?" he said, with a singular look of awe on his face.

"Yes, sir; I am."

I had never seen the man before. He was an elderly man, an American, of whom I knew nothing at all. "I must tell you something strange. I'm not a Christian, but last night I dreamed that to-day a young man would come to tell me the truth of the gospel. When I saw you coming up, I said to myself: 'Yonder is the man.' But you are not a young man; how long have you been a preacher?"

I told him about my conversion, and he said: "You are still young in the gospel."

We talked quite a while over our dinner and after. I prayed with him, and as we parted he said to me: "I have never been a believer; I have been a wicked man; but I believe the gospel, and from this time on I expect to be a better man."

All his talk was in a low, quiet voice. We parted, and I never saw him again and did not even learn his name,

CHAPTER XXII.

GATHERING FRUIT.

THE years I spent on the San Marcos and Luling Missions were years of active work, and many interesting events occurred. I traveled in my hack (covered spring wagon) almost constantly. I had two good horses and a complete camping outfit, and lived among the people. I visited them wherever I found them, and used all kinds of methods to reach them with the gospel. One of the best helps I found to open closed doors was the use of some simple medicines I always carried with me. Medicine has opened many a closed door to me, and people have been much surprised that I gained an entrance that seemed securely closed against the gospel. When I found there was some one sick in the neighborhood, I would go to see him; and if permitted to call, I would give the family the remedy I thought he needed. I made many friends in this way, and many people were reached and converted.

Often, when traveling, I came up with teamsters who were camped for the night, and I camped with them and would talk and preach to them. Often I have put my lantern on the back end of my wagon, and by its light read the Scriptures to the teamsters and preached to them. They always listened to me and were pleased with the singing. In this way I made many friends for the gospel. I have often camped by a field of cotton pickers, and to get an opportunity to talk to them I have taken a sack and picked cotton along with them while I talked of the gospel. I know many of these poor people were saved. I always visited the jails and preached to the prisoners when in the towns, and many souls have heard and believed while in jail.

On one occasion I was going to San Marcos, returning from the country. Along the way I had frequent invitations to stop and spend the night; but I declined them all, moved by an impression that I ought to go on to San Marcos, though I could assign no special reason for doing so. As soon as I reached the town, some friends met me and said: "O, we have been looking for you; there's a sick man here, almost dead, who is asking to see you."

I went to see him at once. When I got in and had spoken to the people, the sick man said: "Don't you know me?"

"No," I said; "I don't."

"I've been in jail," said he; "and because I am about to die they let me out, and I was brought to this house to die. I'm dying. I heard you every time you preached in the jail, and I want you to pray for me."

"And you want me to do it right now, do you?" I asked.

"Yes," said he; "right now."

I read the Scriptures and prayed by his bed. When I got up, I said: "Do you believe in the gospel of our Lord Jesus Christ?"

"Yes, I believe it."

"Will you give me your hand as a sign that you accept Christ as your Saviour?"

He quickly grasped my hand with all his strength. He wanted to be baptized and received into the Church. I did both for him, and he seemed very happy. "O, I am so glad that you came, and that I am now in the militant Church of Christ," he said. People were astonished at the way he rejoiced and talked after he was received as a member of the Church. I left him telling him I was going to fill an appointment and would come back next day to see him. Soon after I left the house he died, and the next day when I returned it was to bury him.

Above the town of Kyle lived the Cruz family. The father was a desperate fighting man, and all the family irreligious but nominally Catholic. I called there one day and said to Mrs. Cruz: "I would like to stop here and preach if you will let me; I'm a minister of the gospel."

You can stop and preach here if you want to; but let me tell you, you need not think you can change my religion."

"O, well, that is the Lord's business. He can change people; I can't."

"Well, you need not think, sir, that I'm going to change; the Lord'll not change me."

I preached; and after I was done, she said to me: "You can come here and preach; but I'll tell you now again, you can't change me."

"Very well," I said; "I can't come here on Sunday to preach, but I'll come once a month on a week night."

I preached there to that family and their neighbors till the end of the year, and at my last appointment I said: "Well, I'm not coming back here any more, so far as I know."

"Why, what's the matter? Why can't you come back?" said Mrs. Cruz.

"I'm going to Conference, and may be sent somewhere else; and, so far as I know, I'll not be back any more."

She began to cry. The tears were rolling down her cheeks, and she was much affected. "O," she said, "I'm so sorry."

It came out that she was nearly ready to join the Church, and she said: "If you don't come back, I'll join the American Church [she and the family spoke English]. Can't I do that?" she asked anxiously.

"Why, yes," I said; "it is just the same; you can join any society you want to." Soon afterwards she joined the American congregation, and is still a member of it, as are several of her children.

I was much interested in the conversion of the wife of Ben Gonzalez, who lived at Gonzalez, Tex. I talked to her much. One day while I was preaching she suddenly sprang up from her seat and ran crying up to the foot of the table that served as my pulpit, and kneeled down there in front of me and cried out: "I want to be baptized right now."

Everybody was much moved and excited. I took her by the hand and lifted her up and said: "Sit down here, sister; I'll attend to it now in a few minutes."

After finishing my sermon I baptized and received her into the Church. She was a splendid woman, lived faithfully, and lately died well.

On the head waters of the Helotes Creek, in Bandera

County, was a man, Juan Morales, a sacristan in the Romish Church. He had frequently said: "I want to talk to Polly Rodriguez. I'll show him his wrong."

One day I went to his house and asked to see him. His wife said that he was not at home; and when I expressed my sorrow that I could not see him, that I was anxious to see him, she said: "If you'll go about a mile up the road, you'll find him killing a beef under a big live oak tree."

I soon found him and went up and shook hands with him and said: "Mr. Morales, I'm sorry to find you so busy in this work, for I wanted to talk with you on the subject of religion."

"The work makes no difference; my boys here can attend to the beef, and we will sit down under the shade of the trees and talk."

We sat down under a tree and began. I had my Bible with me. We talked and argued, and I read the Scriptures. He was a man who had read the Bible and was intelligent; but, like myself before my conversion, he understood nothing he read. We kept up our talk and reading from eight o'clock till two in the afternoon. Then he said: "I'll give it up; you are right and I'm wrong. I'm convinced and I'm a Protestant. Let us go to dinner."

When we got to his house, he said to his wife: "Well, wife, I'm a Protestant."

"What do you say?" she asked with alarm and anger.

He repeated it, and she flew into a terrible passion and said: "Well, if you are, you need not come here." He begged her not to be angry, and to give us some dinner. She did not want to do it, but finally did so, but she was so mad that she would not speak to us nor come near us.

At San Marcos I visited once the family of my cousin, James Tafolla, who was then pastor there. He was absent, but John and Mary, his stepchildren, were present. I read and prayed with them, and I said: "John, why is it that you, a preacher's son, hearing the gospel all the time and knowing it as you do, have not yet believed and confessed Christ?"

As I talked on very kindly to him and Mary the tears began running down his cheeks, and he there and then made his confession. He has since looked upon me as his spiritual father. He is now Rev. Juan J. Mercado, a leading preacher in the Mexican Border Mission Conference.

With this account of the conversion through my instrumentality of a stepson of my kinsman Tafolla, now a brother minister, whom I once insulted and drove out of my house, I will stop. There are many other stories I might tell to show the power of the gospel. I hope this true record of how I was brought to Christ may lead many to believe in him. Perhaps it will preach the gospel when I can no longer do so.

DATE DUE

2 hr. Reserve

Off Reserve

2 hr. Reserve

Off Reserve

AUG 1 4 1995

SEP 0 3 1996

2 hr. Reserve

Off Reserve

2 hr. Reserve

Printed in the USA
CPSIA information can be obtained
at www.ICGtesting.com
LVHW022014290923
759527LV00006B/567